KING DAVID
AND HIS SONGS

KING DAVID
AND HIS SONGS

A STORY OF THE PSALMS

By
Mary Fabyan Windeatt

Illustrated by
Gedge Harmon

TAN BOOKS AND PUBLISHERS, INC.
Rockford, Illinois 61105

Nihil Obstat: Francis J. Reine, S.T.D.
Censor Librorum

Imprimatur: ✠ Paul C. Schulte, D.D.
Archbishop of Indianapolis
Feast of St. Valentine
February 14, 1948

ISBN: 0-89555-429-1

Library of Congress Catalog Card No.: 93-61381

Printed and bound in the United States of America.

TAN BOOKS AND PUBLISHERS, INC.
P. O. Box 424
Rockford, Illinois 61105

1993

For
Marion Swickard.

CONTENTS

ACKNOWLEDGMENTS

The author wishes to thank the Reverend Placidus Kempf, O.S.B., the Reverend Meinrad Hoffman, O.S.B., and the Reverend Conrad Louis, O.S.B., monks of St. Meinrad's Abbey, for their generous help and encouragement in preparing this little story of King David and the Psalms.

PSALMS QUOTED IN THIS BOOK

PUBLISHER'S NOTE

In this book the Psalms are quoted in the Douay-Rheims translation, using the numbering system of the Douay-Rheims version of the Bible.*

---

* For example, the Psalm which is called Psalm 23 in modern translations, which are based on the Hebrew, is Psalm 22 in the Douay-Rheims, which is based on the Latin Vulgate. The divergence in numbering begins in the middle of Psalm 9 (Douay-Rheims version).

KING DAVID
AND HIS SONGS

CHAPTER 1

THE SECRET ANOINTING

A BOUT ONE thousand years before the birth of Our Lord, there lived near Bethlehem a man named Isai (also known as Jesse). He had eight sons whom he loved dearly, especially the youngest, a boy of 15 whose name was David.

Now one day Isai was astonished to learn that Samuel, the holy prophet of the Hebrew people, had come to see him.

"What can the great Samuel want of me?" Isai asked a bit nervously of the servant who brought the news. "What have I done?"

"I don't know sir," replied the servant. "But I think that the prophet comes on peaceful business."

Isai lost no time in gathering together his household—his wife, his servants and the seven oldest boys. All must come with him to greet Samuel, and to wish him well. But he did not bother to summon David, who was away in the fields tending the sheep, for the boy was little more than a child, and Isai thought it unlikely that the great prophet would be interested in seeing him.

1

But in this he was mistaken. "Let me see this youngest son," Samuel commanded. So a servant was dispatched to summon David from the fields and to find someone else to watch the sheep.

Now when the servant came upon Isai's youngest boy, he found him sitting under a tree playing upon a little wooden flute. All about him the flocks were grazing peacefully, and in the branches of the tree overhead the birds were making music of their own—echoes of the youthful shepherd's happy tune. It was a pleasant sight, but the servant did not pause to enjoy it.

"Young master, you must come at once!" he cried breathlessly. "The great and holy prophet Samuel is here and wants to see you!"

David looked up in surprise. "The holy prophet wants to see *me?*"

"Yes, young master."

David laid down his flute. "All right," he said. "I'll come."

When David was brought before Samuel, the prophet's heart swelled with joy. What a fine-looking boy this was! Even more important, his clear gaze and courteous manners proclaimed him to be a lad whom one could trust—truthful, obedient, willing.

"Come here, my son," said Samuel.

Puzzled yet eager, David approached Samuel. Then the latter took some holy oil, offered a brief prayer and anointed David's head.

"May the Lord bless you," he said.

Everyone present was full of wonder. What was

the meaning of this action of the holy prophet? Only kings were anointed with oil. And there was already a king ruling over Israel—Saul. But when asked for an explanation, Samuel had only one answer. What had just happened was to be kept a secret. And if anyone wanted to know the reason for Samuel's presence at Isai's house, he was to be told that the prophet had come to offer sacrifice to God. This would be true, for Samuel had brought with him a young calf which even now, according to the Hebrew custom, his assistants were making ready to be slain.

The next day all was as usual at Isai's house. Father and sons were busy at their various tasks, with David out in the fields watching the sheep. Naturally the boy could not help pondering the strange events of the day before, but soon he was busy at his favorite pastime, playing the flute. He knew many songs, some handed down from one generation to another, others which he had composed himself.

"I believe I'll sing one of my own little songs," he decided. And laying down the flute, he began to consider which it should be. Then suddenly he knew. It would be one of his favorites, a song which always had brought peace to his heart when he was troubled. He had sung it many times, especially when out of doors tending the flocks. Now he would sing it again, and perhaps it would drive away the little cloud of anxiety which had been produced by the prophet Samuel's visit and lingered to trouble his heart whenever he thought of

THE YOUNG SHEPHERD KNEW MANY SONGS.

the strange thing that the holy man had done in anointing him with oil.

So David lifted his clear, young voice in song, a song of trust and confidence in God:

> The Lord ruleth me: and I shall want nothing. He hath set me in a place of pasture.
>
> He hath brought me up, on the water of refreshment: he hath converted my soul.
>
> He hath led me on the paths of justice, for his own name's sake.
>
> For though I should walk in the midst of the shadow of death, I will fear no evils, for thou art with me.
>
> Thy rod and thy staff, they have comforted me.
>
> Thou hast prepared a table before me against them that afflict me.
>
> Thou hast anointed my head with oil; and my chalice which inebriateth *me*, how goodly is it!
>
> And thy mercy will follow me all the days of my life.
>
> And that I may dwell in the house of the Lord unto length of days.*

Psalm 22

"SOON THE KING MAY FEEL BETTER,"
THOUGHT DAVID.

6

CHAPTER 2

IN THE HOUSEHOLD OF KING SAUL

AVID COULD play other instruments than the flute. In fact, as he grew older he became well known throughout the countryside for his ability as a musician. Then one day an invitation came from the royal household. Would David come to play and sing for King Saul? The king was not well. Indeed, sometimes it seemed as though an evil spirit were troubling him. He could not sleep or eat. And for days at a time he would be filled with such gloom that he could not attend to his duties.

"Of course I'll play and sing for the king," David said eagerly. "Perhaps my little songs will make him feel better."

So off David went, pleased and excited at the prospect of rendering a service to his ruler.

Now as soon as the king had laid eyes upon his visitor, his spirits lifted. What a likable young boy was this shepherd from Bethlehem! And if it were true that he was also a skilled musician...

"Give the lad a harp and let us hear what he can

7

do," he told his servants.

So in just a little while, amid the splendor and luxury of the royal court, David was busy at what he loved so well—playing and singing. And since something told him that the reason for the king's sadness of heart was that he prayed to God so rarely, the boy decided to sing a song that was all about God's greatness and glory, a composition of his own which had brought great pleasure to his friends and neighbors. He thought for a moment and then began:

> O Lord our Lord, how admirable is thy name in the whole earth!
>
> For thy magnificence is elevated above the heavens.
>
> Out of the mouth of infants and of sucklings thou hast perfected praise, because of thy enemies, that thou mayst destroy the enemy and the avenger.
>
> For I will behold thy heavens, the works of thy fingers: the moon and the stars which thou hast founded.
>
> What is man that thou art mindful of him? or the son of man that thou visitest him?
>
> Thou hast made him a little less than the angels, thou hast crowned him with glory and honour: and hast set him over the works of thy hands.
>
> Thou hast subjected all things under his feet, all sheep and oxen: moreover the beasts also of the fields.
>
> The birds of the air, and the fishes of the sea, that pass through the paths of the sea.

O Lord our Lord, how admirable is thy name
in all the earth!*

King Saul was carried out of himself at David's fine
voice, as well as by his skill upon the harp. "You must
stay here with me," he declared. "I'll pay you well
and make you my armor-bearer. What do you say?"

What was there to say? David fully realized the
honor which was being given to him, as well as to
his whole family, by the generous offer of the king.
"Of course I'll stay, sire," he replied gratefully, "and
for as long as you wish."

So David left his home near Bethlehem and
came to live in the royal household. In a short while
he had made friends with everyone, including Jonathan, King Saul's son. The two spent many happy
hours together, and sometimes David played and
sang for Jonathan as well as for his father. A few
people marveled that a prince and a shepherd
should be such close friends, but the wise men of
the court understood. David might be of lowly
birth, but his spirit was a noble one. He was honest,
loyal, willing, and by his music he had accom-
plished what no one else in the kingdom had been
able to do. He had restored some measure of peace
and joy to the troubled heart of the king.

"David and his songs are worth far more than
gold," the wise men told one another. "See how
King Saul has improved in health and spirits since
the lad came here to live!"

---

*Psalm 8

CHAPTER 3

THE FEARSOME GIANT

SOON EVERYONE in the royal family loved David. Never had they known such a skilled musician as this shepherd boy from Bethlehem. Finally, however, David felt that he ought to go home. His father was growing old and had need of him. Perhaps he might return, even if only for a visit?

"Yes, you may go," said the king. "You have served me faithfully and deserve a rest from your duties."

So David returned to his family and once more took up his old task of caring for the flocks. In his time at court he had written many new songs and had grown more expert than ever at playing upon the harp and flute. But what surprised everyone was his unusual strength. If a wild beast ventured to bear down upon the flock, David never dreamed of running away or of letting it harm a single sheep. He would fling himself upon the savage creature and hold its throat in the strong grasp of his hands until it was dead.

"The lad strangled a lion in this fashion," said one man admiringly.

"Yes, and he killed a bear in the same way," replied another.

"He'll make a fine soldier when he grows older," declared a third.

David was glad that he had strength and courage as well as the skill to make up songs and to play upon the harp and flute. But well he knew that these things are gifts from God, and that he himself had never done anything to merit them.

"Dear Lord, thank You for Your gifts," he often prayed. "And help me to use them in Your service."

Now at that time war broke out between the Hebrews and a godless race of people known as the Philistines. David's older brothers went off to battle, for King Saul needed every able-bodied man to help him defend the country. David, however, was left at home.

"You shall look after our father," said the older brothers. "He's an old man now, and someone must stay with him."

David accepted the charge willingly, but his heart was sad that his people were at war. How dreadful if the Philistines should be victorious! Then he and all his relatives would be made slaves.

"I wish that I could do something," he often thought. "But what *can* I do, for surely I cannot leave my duties here?"

Then one day David's father sent him on an unexpected errand. "Go to the battlefield and see how things are with your brothers," he commanded.

"Take some food with you, too. It wouldn't do for
my boys to be hungry."

So David hurried off to where the armies of
Israel and of the Philistines were encamped—
taking with him some bread, cheese and other
things that his brothers liked. But when he arrived,
he was surprised to discover that no battle was taking place. Instead, the two armies were drawn up
in the mountains, with a wide valley between them,
still making preparations for the approaching conflict. But even more surprising was the report concerning a great hulk of a man named Goliath, who
left his Philistine comrades each morning and evening to parade up and down in the valley, shouting
insults to the whole Hebrew army.

"Cowards! Let one of you come down and fight
with me!" he would boast. "We'll soon see who's
the winner!"

David was all eyes and ears. "Has anyone offered
to go and fight this man?" he asked eagerly of an
old soldier.

The latter stared in amazement. "Of course not,
boy! Why, Goliath is more than nine feet tall! It
would be certain death for anyone to go out against
him."

Presently David saw for himself the boastful
giant who came down each morning and evening
into the valley to challenge the men of Israel to single combat. Reluctantly he admitted that Goliath
was the biggest and the strongest man he had ever
seen. Why, his armor alone must weigh several hundred pounds! Yet how terrible! If no one took up

his challenge, in a little while there would be a dreadful battle. Thousands of men would lose their lives. Perhaps even his own brothers would be killed!

"Suppose I go out against him," he suggested one day. "I have a plan of attack that might work."

His remark was not taken seriously. If the strongest men of Israel knew that they had not the slightest chance against Goliath, how could a mere boy talk of victory?

But David was much in earnest. "Let me go!" he pleaded. "You've heard what the Philistine says: 'Choose out a man of you, and let him come down and fight hand to hand. If he be able to fight with me, and kill me, we will be servants to you.'"

David's brothers were really angered by his offer to go out against Goliath. In their opinion it was a piece of boastful stupidity.

"Get back to our father's flocks!" they ordered. "You know nothing at all about fighting."

David did not give up hope, however, and finally he succeeded in obtaining an interview with King Saul. Eagerly he repeated his offer to fight the giant, explaining that he was very strong, despite his youth. Why, he had even strangled wild beasts with his bare hands when they had attacked his father's flocks! And surely it would be a wonderful thing if he should kill Goliath? Then the war would be over, and there would be peace.

Saul smiled at the boy who had played so often for him upon the harp and flute and whose skill in setting beautiful words to music was without

"LET ME GO OUT AGAINST THE GIANT!"

equal. "My son, you are not able to withstand this Philistine," he said kindly, "nor to fight against him. You are but a boy, and he is a warrior from his youth."

"My lord, He Who delivered me out of the paw of the lion, and out of the paw of the bear, will deliver me out of the hand of this Philistine," replied David confidently.

In spite of himself King Saul was impressed, and finally he spoke the words which David had been awaiting so eagerly. "Very well," he said. "Tomorrow you may fight Goliath. Go, and the Lord be with you."

That night David prepared for battle in a fashion that astonished everyone. He took a harp and began to sing! But not an ordinary song. No, like so many of the young shepherd's songs, this one was really a prayer—a prayer for help and strength in the approaching conflict:

> The Lord is my light and my salvation, whom shall I fear?
> The Lord is the protector of my life: of whom shall I be afraid?
> Whilst the wicked draw near against me, to eat my flesh.
> My enemies that trouble me, have themselves been weakened, and have fallen.
> If armies in camp should stand together against me, my heart shall not fear.
> If a battle should rise up against me, in this will I be confident.
> One thing I have asked of the Lord, this will

I seek after; that I may dwell in the house of the Lord all the days of my life.

That I may see the delight of the Lord, and may visit his temple.

For he hath hidden me in his tabernacle; in the day of evils, he hath protected me in the secret place of his tabernacle.

He hath exalted me upon a rock: and now he hath lifted up my head above my enemies.

I have gone round, and have offered up in his tabernacle a sacrifice of jubilation: I will sing, and recite a psalm to the Lord.

Hear, O Lord, my voice, with which I have cried to thee: have mercy on me and hear me.

My heart hath said to thee: My face hath sought thee: thy face, O Lord, will I still seek.

Turn not away thy face from me; decline not in thy wrath from thy servant.

Be thou my helper, forsake me not; do not thou despise me, O God my Saviour.

For my father and my mother have left me: but the Lord hath taken me up.

Set me, O Lord, a law in thy way, and guide me in the right path, because of my enemies.

Deliver me not over to the will of them that trouble me; for unjust witnesses have risen up against me; and iniquity hath lied to itself.

I believe to see the good things of the Lord in the land of the living.

Expect the Lord, do manfully, and let thy heart take courage, and wait thou for the Lord.*

---

*Psalm 26

CHAPTER 4

DAVID AND GOLIATH

THE NEXT morning Saul commanded that David be clothed in his own fine armor and girded with the royal sword. All precautions were to be taken to protect his life. But when David put on the king's armor, he found that it was far too heavy.

"I'm not used to such a weight," he told the king. "Why, I can hardly walk!" Then he took off the armor, laid aside the royal sword and picked up his shepherd's staff.

"This is much better," he announced. And having found five small stones in a nearby brook, he placed them in the shepherd's bag that hung about his neck and started down to the valley.

As usual, Goliath was parading up and down, shouting insults to the Hebrew forces. Where was the man who could defeat him in battle? Why, nowhere! Such a man had never been born! But as soon as he saw David approaching, his boastfulness gave place to violent rage.

"They've sent a *boy* to fight me!" he roared.

17

"THEY'VE SENT A BOY TO FIGHT ME!" HE ROARED.

"And with just a staff in his hand! Am I a dog, then? Come close, lad, and I'll give your flesh to the birds of the air and to the beasts of the earth!"

David looked at the nine-foot giant. His head was encased in a brass helmet, his body fitted with glittering armor, and in his hand was an enormous spear. The sight of him should have dismayed the stoutest heart, but the boy's gaze did not waver.

"You come to me with a sword, and with a spear, and with a shield," he called out fearlessly, "but I come to you in the name of the Lord of hosts, the God of the armies of Israel, which you have defied."

The giant bared his teeth. "You say this—to *me?*"

David grasped his shepherd's staff more firmly. "Yes. And much more. This day the Lord will deliver you into my hand, and I will cut off your head. And I will give the bodies of your men to the birds of the air, and to the beasts of the earth: that all the earth may know that there is a God in Israel."

This was too much for the giant. With great strides he came across the valley, his armor-bearer toiling after him, while the armies of Israel and of the Philistines watched with bated breath.

"Death to you, miserable boy!" roared the giant. "A wretched death!"

Grief-stricken, King Saul covered his eyes. "I should never have let the lad go," he muttered. "Never! Never!"

In the brilliance of the morning sun the armor of the Philistine flashed like fire, and suddenly David appeared pitifully small and weak to all observers. Why, his head barely reached Goliath's elbow! Surely in a moment he would lie dead—crushed by one blow from his fearsome enemy? But even as the two armies watched, the youthful shepherd drew a stone from the bag hanging from his neck, fitted it into a sling, and sent it whizzing through the air straight at Goliath.

There was a horrible scream, like that of a wounded beast. The giant halted abruptly, staggered for a moment, then fell heavily on his back with his shield and spear on top of him.

At once astonished cries arose from the Hebrew armies. "He's dead! Goliath's dead!"

"No! No!" cried the Philistines. "It can't be!"

But Goliath was dead. David's stone, shot skillfully from the sling, was buried deep in his forehead.

"Thank You, Lord," whispered David, as he ran forward to stand over his fallen enemy. "Thank You for Your help!" Then, since he had no sword of his own, he took up that of Goliath, and in a moment he had cut off the giant's head.

Realizing now that the dreadful enemy really was dead, the Hebrew armies were fearful no longer. With joyful cries they raced down the mountain to the valley, then up to the enemy camp on the opposite side. "Death to the Philistines!" they shouted. "Death to all those who have insulted our God!"

Of course David was very happy—particularly later in the day when he learned that his comrades had pursued the bewildered Philistines so successfully that now the war was over. But when King

Saul sought to congratulate him and to praise him for his bravery, he shook his head.

"My lord, today's victory belongs to God," he said. "Without His help, I could have done nothing."

At such humble words, the king's admiration mounted to new heights. "My son, you must come to live with me," he declared. "Watching sheep is no fit task for a warrior."

A wave of applause greeted this remark. "Yes, David must be one of us," agreed the soldiers. "There's never been such a brave youth in all Israel."

"And we'll celebrate his victory with a great banquet," put in Jonathan, the king's son, eagerly. "There'll be food and wine for everyone. And David will play and sing for us."

King Saul smiled. "That's right," he said. "When a war is won, there is always a celebration. And what is a celebration without music?"

So a great banquet was arranged, and David was the guest of honor. But when the king pressed him to tell of his victory in a new song, the young hero begged to be excused. He would sing an old song instead, a song in praise of Him by Whose power alone the Philistines had been conquered.

"Very well," said Saul, smiling. "Sing us your old song."

Bowing humbly, David took the harp which a servant brought him, ran his fingers lightly over the strings, and began:

I will praise thee, O Lord, with my whole heart: for thou hast heard the words of my mouth.

I will sing praise to thee in the sight of the angels: I will worship towards thy holy temple, and I will give glory to thy name.

For thy mercy, and for thy truth: for thou hast magnified thy holy name above all.

In what day soever I shall call upon thee, hear me: thou shalt multiply strength in my soul.

May all the kings of the earth give glory to thee: for they have heard all the words of thy mouth.

And let them sing in the ways of the Lord: for great is the glory of the Lord.

For the Lord is high, and looketh on the low: and the high he knoweth afar off.

If I shall walk in the midst of tribulation, thou wilt quicken me: and thou hast stretched forth thy hand against the wrath of my enemies: and thy right hand hath saved me.

The Lord will repay for me: thy mercy, O Lord, endureth for ever: O despise not the works of thy hands.*

*Psalm 137

CHAPTER 5

LOVE TURNS TO HATRED

IN THE days that followed, David was treated as a true hero. Whenever he appeared in the streets, the people greeted him with smiles and words of praise. King Saul was a great warrior, they said. To protect his country he had risked his life against thousands of men. But in meeting Goliath and killing him, David had done much more.

"Saul has slain his thousands, and David his tens of thousands!" was the universal cry. "All honor to the young shepherd of Bethlehem!"

"I value this boy's friendship above all things," declared Prince Jonathan. "He is closer to me than a brother."

"And I love him with my whole heart," the young Princess Michol, Saul's daughter, secretly confessed. "Oh, how I envy my older sister Merob, who will probably be his wife!"

At first King Saul was pleased at David's popularity. He took great satisfaction in recalling that it had been he who was wise enough to give the boy a chance to show his skill as a warrior, then to put him in an important place in the army. But as time passed, his feelings changed. Instead of rejoicing in the honor shown to David, he grew jealous. He was especially displeased when the boy was greeted with hearty applause by the people in the streets.

"Listen to them!" he would mutter. "'Saul has slain his thousands, and David his tens of thousands!' Have they forgotten that I am the king? And that I know far more about warfare than this ignorant shepherd?"

Daily Saul's jealousy increased, until finally a real and terrible hatred filled his heart. Most of his time was spent in planning how he could harm the youth whom he had once loved and cherished. He became moody and sullen and would neither eat nor drink.

"Alas, the king is suffering from his old disease," declared one of the wise men of the court, ignorant of the true state of affairs. "It's the same that plagued him when we first brought the shepherd boy here to play and sing his songs."

"In that case perhaps David should spare a little time from his new duties to play and sing for the king again," suggested a companion. "Remember how his music used to soothe him and make him feel better?"

So it was that David left his work in the army and daily came before the king with his harp or flute. To the best of his ability he tried to cheer the melancholy Saul, little knowing that it was he himself who was the cause of such low spirits. And though for hours at a time enchanting notes of song filled the room where the king sat glumly on his throne, holding his spear and staring vacantly into space, the joyous music was to no avail. Not even David's fine voice or his wonderful skill upon stringed instruments could overcome the evil spirit which now reigned in the king's heart.

"My lord, what is the matter?" the young musician asked anxiously one day. "What is troubling you?"

The king glared. "Nothing," he muttered. "Nothing."

"But there must be something! Why, you no longer walk about or talk to your people. And you won't eat or drink. . ."

"What is that to you?" roared Saul. And suddenly reaching for his spear, he cast it fiercely in David's direction.

Quickly the latter stepped aside, so that the spear buried itself harmlessly in the wall behind him. Then, as though nothing had happened, he began to play a soothing melody on the harp. But his self-control only made Saul the angrier. "Are you afraid of nothing?" he screamed. "Get out! And take your music with you! I'm sick and tired of listening to it!"

By now David realized the truth—that he could do nothing to help his sovereign. For some strange reason King Saul hated him and would kill him if he could.

"Yet what have I done?" he asked himself miserably. "Surely I've been a loyal subject? Surely I've tried to please everyone since I came to live here?"

KING SAUL WOULD KILL HIM IF HE COULD!

Even as David stood pondering, the king seized a second spear and sent it flying at his head. "Didn't you hear me?" he bellowed. "Go! And take your harp with you!"

Bowing low, David obeyed the royal command. But his heart was heavy as he sought his own quarters. What a terrible trial had suddenly come his way! For the first time in his life a friend had turned against him!

"But why?" he murmured brokenly. "*Why?*"

Then, as had been his custom since childhood, he fell to his knees and began to pour out his sorrow in prayer—humbly asking for help and courage:

> O God, come to my assistance; O Lord, make haste to help me.
>
> Let them be confounded and ashamed that seek my soul:
>
> Let them be turned backward, and blush for shame that desire evils to me:
>
> Let them be presently turned away blushing for shame that say to me: 'T is well, 't is well.
>
> Let all that seek thee rejoice and be glad in thee; and let such as love thy salvation say always: The Lord be magnified.
>
> But I am needy and poor; O God, help me.
>
> Thou art my helper and my deliverer: O Lord, make no delay.*

Psalm 69

CHAPTER 6

DAVID'S LIFE IN DANGER

D AY BY day Saul grew more envious of David, but for the most part he managed to keep his evil thoughts to himself. In fact, to please the people and to set himself up as an honest man, he decided to keep a promise that he had made long ago: namely that as the victor over Goliath, David should have the Princess Merob, his oldest daughter, for his wife. Yet in the depths of his heart, he continued to wish the young shepherd all possible harm.

"May the hands of the Philistines be upon him," he muttered. "May they take him, and put him to death!"

Although David knew that the king no longer loved him, he never measured the full extent of his hatred in the wildest of his imaginings. Thus, when Saul suddenly broke his word and declared that Merob should not be David's wife after all, but her younger sister Michol, he did not take offense. Who was he—a poor and ignorant shepherd—to decide what should or should not be done in matters per-

28

taining to the royal family?

"The young man is really sincere and honest," Saul's advisers reported. "We have talked with him as you commanded, and it is plain to see that he is just as happy at the thought of marrying one princess as another—since it is your will."

Saul's eyes were crafty. "Ah, but doesn't he hold a grudge against me because I have given the Princess Merob to another?"

"Oh, no, sire."

"Well, then, he's doing everything possible to win the people's affection. He goes out among them daily, pretending to be wise and virtuous so that they will take away my throne and make him king."

Puzzled, the advisers looked at one another. Then slowly they shook their heads. "David has done none of these things, sire. He is one of your most loyal subjects."

Suddenly Saul's jealousy burst its bonds. Calling together his family and servants, he informed them that David must be slain, for beneath his winning ways, his songs and ready wit, he was at heart a traitor.

"Rid me of this miserable youth and your reward shall be truly great!" he cried. "I promise it!"

At these words everyone was aghast, particularly Prince Jonathan. His dear friend David a traitor? Impossible! Why, since his first days at court he had been honest and kind in all his dealings, and utterly without pride. Not even his wonderful victory over Goliath, or the extravagant praise of the people, had turned his head.

"Father, you're dreadfully mistaken," Jonathan declared earnestly, when he and King Saul were alone. "Why, if need be David would give his life for you, or for me, or for our people. Don't you know that?"

Stubbornly the king shook his head. "He wants the throne," he muttered. "I can see it in his eyes."

"No, he doesn't, Father. Oh, surely you've not forgotten how he risked his life against Goliath and saved thousands of men from dying in battle? You saw him fight the giant on that day, and you were so proud of him! Now, how can you possibly think of killing him?"

So eagerly did Jonathan plead David's cause that finally King Saul relented. He admitted that perhaps he had misjudged the youthful shepherd. Perhaps he was not a traitor after all. In such a case, it would be a very grave sin to take his life.

"Then you'll forgive and forget, Father? You'll tell your men not to touch David?"

Slowly the king nodded. "For your sake, my son, I'll tell them," he said.

Saul kept his word, and presently David was restored to his former works. Jonathan rejoiced at this, for he loved the youth from Bethlehem as he had never loved another human being. In fact, long ago he had paid him the great honor of bestowing upon him his own royal garments, including his sword and other weapons of war.

"Before God, you are my best friend in all the world," he had declared solemnly. "I swear it."

"And you are mine," David had replied humbly.

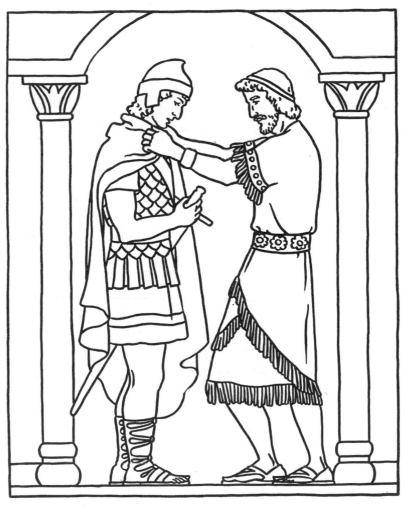

JONATHAN GAVE DAVID HIS OWN ROYAL GARMENTS.

Others in the royal household likewise rejoiced that once more King Saul was looking favorably upon David. And when a new war broke out with the Philistines and the young shepherd covered himself with fresh glory on the battlefield, his name was on every tongue.

"There's never been such a great soldier in all our history," one person told another excitedly. "The Lord gives David victory wherever he goes."

"Yes," was the reply. "And still he remains plain and simple. He never sets himself up as a hero."

Saul was well aware of what the people were saying, and of David's growing popularity, and finally the old jealousy asserted itself. Day after day he would fall into terrible fits of melancholy from which he could scarcely be roused.

"Perhaps a little music would help the king," suggested the wise men of the court. "David, will you take your harp and play and sing for him?"

"Willingly," replied David. And in the simplicity of his soul, he decided upon a song about a just man—one worthy to enter the temple and pray there to God:

Lord, who shall dwell in thy tabernacle? or who shall rest in thy holy hill?

He that walketh without blemish, and worketh justice:

He that speaketh truth in his heart, who hath not used deceit in his tongue:

Nor hath done evil to his neighbour: nor taken up a reproach against his neighbours.

In his sight the malignant is brought to nothing: but he glorifieth them that fear the Lord.

He that sweareth to his neighbour, and deceiveth not; he that hath not put out his money to usury, nor taken bribes against the innocent:

He that doth these things shall not be moved for ever.*

Seated upon his throne, his head drooped low upon his chest, his spear held limply in his hand, Saul gave no sign of hearing David's song. To all appearances he was as a man sunk in slumber—or deep sorrow. Then suddenly a violent shaking seized his limbs. With a mad scream he rose unsteadily to his feet, lifted his spear and cast it furiously in David's direction.

"Wretch!" he cried, his eyes glittering. "You dare to sing such a song to me? To heap reproaches upon my head?"

As on the earlier occasion, David succeeded in dodging the deadly weapon. But this time he made no effort to soothe his master. He merely took his harp and slipped quietly from the room, his heart filled with the pain of a terrible realization:

"The king hasn't changed after all!" he whispered. "He still hates me to the death!"

*Psalm 14

CHAPTER 7

DAVID GOES TO THE PHILISTINES

THAT NIGHT, in the privacy of his own quarters, David's heart grew still heavier. No matter from which door or window he looked, he could see men moving about in the darkness, and the glint of swords and spears. As for the Princess Michol—who for some time now had been David's beloved wife—she was beside herself with anxiety.

"Father's posted an armed guard about the house!" she cried. "Oh, David! You must flee at once!"

David looked at his beautiful young wife, then hid his face in his hands. "But what have I done to be treated like a criminal?" he cried brokenly.

"Nothing! Nothing! But I beg you to go at once! If you stay here, the soldiers will surely take you prisoner. And by tomorrow. . ."

"By tomorrow I'll be dead!"

"Yes. And it mustn't be that way. Quick, there's a window over the courtyard. . ."

"*What?* You'd have me run off like a coward?"

"OH, DAVID! YOU MUST FLEE AT ONCE!"

"There's nothing else to do, David! Not until I have the chance to plead with Father. Oh, hurry! Get out of the city before it's too late!"

Recognizing the wisdom in Michol's words, David finally agreed to go. With a brief but loving farewell for his loyal young wife, he slipped through a window into the courtyard, and by a stroke of good luck he succeeded in evading the king's soldiers and making his way unnoticed through the dark and deserted streets.

"Michol is right," he told himself presently. "I must get as far away from the city as possible. Only in the country will I have any real chance to escape the king's men."

All that night David traveled, knowing for the first time in his life the dreadful agony of being hunted as though he were a wild beast. Not even a visit with the holy prophet Samuel, who lived in Ramatha, some miles distant, brought any lasting peace. King Saul desired his life. Nowhere in Israel was he safe.

"Perhaps Jonathan could help me again," he thought. "Oh, if I could have just a few words with him!"

The days passed, and David moved about the countryside in constant fear of his life. But when he finally succeeded in meeting Jonathan, the young prince had little consolation to offer.

"Dearest friend, Father is terribly bitter towards you," he declared sorrowfully. "I've made every effort to reason with him, but he won't listen. Why, he even threw his spear at me when I tried to tell him of your loyalty!"

"Then I have to remain in hiding?"

"Yes—at least for a while."

What else was there to say? After a renewal of their pledge of loyalty the two friends parted— Jonathan for home, David for the nearby city of Nobe. By now he was very tired and weak from hunger. Surely it would be wise to seek refuge with Achimelech the high priest? Saul's men, even the most bloodthirsty, would never dare to cross the threshold of a consecrated servant of God.

Yet soon even this scheme seemed a hopeless one, and when David reached Achimelech's house he had not the courage to explain his situation truthfully. Instead, he told the high priest that he was journeying on important business for King Saul, and that in his haste he had come away without a sword or sufficient provisions. Achimelech, entirely unaware of the fact that there was a price on David's head, readily agreed to supply him with what he needed.

"You'll stay and visit a while in Nobe?" he asked eagerly. "There are many here who would be honored to meet the king's son-in-law."

David shook his head regretfully. "No," he said. "The king's business is urgent. I must be on my way."

When he had taken his departure, however, the young fugitive experienced fresh uneasiness. First, he had told several lies to the high priest. Second, he had certainly been seen in Nobe by a man who could cause him much trouble. This was Doeg, chief herdsman to King Saul.

"Things are becoming really desperate," he told himself sadly. "Oh, what am I going to do?"

From earliest boyhood David had turned to God in time of trouble, relying upon His strength instead of his own for a solution to all difficulties. But now he foolishly set aside his customary practice.

"God has forgotten me, so what's the use of praying to Him?" he thought. "And since I've lied to the high priest, there's no harm in lying to other men."

Deep down within him his heart cried out that this was not so. But David would not listen, and finally he made a fatal decision. To save his own life, he would abandon his people. He would go to the Philistines and offer his services against King Saul. In many ways this might appear to be a cowardly and treacherous course of action, but what other lay open, he asked himself. And perhaps in time he could trick the Philistines and use his experience with them to the advantage of his own people.

In a short while the plan had been put into effect. David entered the land of the Philistines, was captured, then brought before King Achis.

"Your Majesty, we've discovered a dangerous enemy!" cried the royal servants excitedly. "What shall we do with him?"

King Achis looked at the newly arrived prisoner —his clothes torn, his face covered with grime, his hair and beard wild and matted.

"A dangerous enemy?" he exclaimed unbelievingly. *"This man?"*

"Yes, Your Majesty. Don't you know him? He's David, the son-in-law of King Saul."

"Not the one who killed our great Goliath?"

"Yes, Your Majesty. The very same."

Suddenly a murmur of angry voices arose in the court, and David felt his courage fail. Oh, how foolish he had been to enter the land of the Philistines! Presently he would be given over to the torturers! There would be no chance at all to convince King Achis that he had come to seek safety at his court. . .that quite innocently he had incurred the wrath of his own sovereign. . .

"No! No!" he cried frantically. "I'm not David! I'm an old man. . .a sick man. . ." And falling to his knees, he glared wildly from one face to another. Then before anyone could stop him he was rolling upon the ground in a pretended fit of madness.

For a moment Achis stared in amazement. Then he turned away abruptly. "You saw that the man was mad," he told his attendants in a disgusted tone. "Why have you brought him to me?"

"But Your Majesty. . ."

"Have we need of madmen, that you have brought in this fellow to play the madman in my presence? Take him away at once!"

The attendants dared not argue. Grasping David by the arms, they dragged him roughly from the royal presence and cast him into the street.

"Be off, fool!" they cried. "Take your antics someplace else."

For several minutes David lay prostrate in the dust where he had fallen. Then slowly he raised himself. "Oh, Lord, how can I thank You?" he whispered. "You have saved my life once more!"

By now a curious crowd had gathered about, but David paid them little heed. He was free! Free to return to his own country! Oh, how else could he express himself save in song—a song that was really a prayer of thanksgiving:

I will bless the Lord at all times, his praise shall be always in my mouth.

In the Lord shall my soul be praised: let the meek hear and rejoice.

O magnify the Lord with me; and let us extol his name together.

I sought the Lord, and he heard me; and he delivered me from all my troubles.

Come ye to him and be enlightened: and your faces shall not be confounded.

This poor man cried, and the Lord heard him: and saved him out of all his troubles.

The angel of the Lord shall encamp round about them that fear him: and shall deliver them.

O taste, and see that the Lord is sweet: blessed is the man that hopeth in him.

Fear the Lord, all ye his saints: for there is no want to them that fear him.

The rich have wanted, and have suffered hunger: but they that seek the Lord shall not be deprived of any good.

Come, children, hearken to me: I will teach you the fear of the Lord.

Who is the man that desireth life: who loveth to see good days?

Keep thy tongue from evil, and thy lips from speaking guile.

Turn away from evil and do good: seek after peace and pursue it.

The eyes of the Lord are upon the just: and his ears unto their prayers.

But the countenance of the Lord is against them that do evil things: to cut off the remembrance of them from the earth.

The just cried, and the Lord heard them: and delivered them out of all their troubles.

The Lord is nigh unto them that are of a contrite heart: and he will save the humble of spirit.

Many are the afflictions of the just; but out of them all will the Lord deliver them.

The Lord keepeth all their bones, not one of them shall be broken.

The death of the wicked is very evil: and they that hate the just shall be guilty.

The Lord will redeem the souls of his servants: and none of them that trust in him shall offend.*

*Psalm 33

CHAPTER 8

FLEEING FROM KING SAUL

DAVID LOST no time in leaving the land of the Philistines, and finally he established himself in a large cave near Bethlehem. Learning this, many men came to offer their services, for they had known David since childhood and were grieved at the treatment given to him by King Saul. Now, they suggested, he no longer need be alone in his troubles.

"There are 400 of us, sir," declared one young man earnestly. "And each of us would gladly die rather than let the king's men touch a hair of your head."

David was grateful to have so many friends, although he worried about his family—his aged parents, his brothers and sisters. It was all very well for him to lead a roving life, ever on the watch for the soldiers of King Saul. But surely his dear ones should not be subjected to such hardship?

"I think that we had better go to the land of Moab," he announced one day. "There my family can surely live in peace."

So David and his followers left the cave near Bethlehem and set out for Moab—a country on the east side of the Dead Sea—where the local ruler promised to protect David's relations for the rest of their days.

Life was pleasant in Moab, and David would not have minded remaining there indefinitely. But one day a message arrived from the holy prophet Samuel, brought by a disciple named Gad. The king's son-in-law, regardless of the price upon his head, must return to his own country at once. There was work for him to do.

Obediently David and his followers set out for home. But after much thought and discussion, they decided against returning to the cave near Bethlehem. Instead they would go to the forest of Haret, some miles distant. King Saul would be less apt to look for them there.

Not long after their arrival, a young man entered the forest and begged protection from David's band. This was Abiathar, the son of Achimelech, the high priest of Nobe. But what a change had come over the youth since anyone had last seen him! Now he was ragged, pale and on the verge of starvation.

"You're in trouble, Abiathar!" cried David anxiously. "What's happened? Why aren't you with your father in Nobe?"

Tears filled Abiathar's eyes. "My father is dead," he replied.

"*Dead?*"

"Yes. And my whole family, too."

"But I don't understand!"

"WHAT'S HAPPENED? CRIED DAVID ANXIOUSLY.

"King Saul found out that Father helped you on your journey to the Philistines, sir, and commanded that he be punished by death, and all the people of Nobe as well. Doeg, the king's herdsman, led the attack."

"And you—"

"With great difficulty I escaped. Now, if you'll have me, I'd like to join your little company."

Willingly David received the high priest's son into his company, promising him every assistance. But his heart was heavy at the thought of the terrible things which had happened at Nobe.

"If only I hadn't lied to this boy's father!" he told himself remorsefully. "The high priest never knew that I was an outlaw. And now he and hundreds of other innocent souls have suffered death for my sake! Oh, what a sad day that was when Doeg saw me at Achimelech's house!"

In the midst of David's sorrow, word reached him that the city of Ceila was being fiercely attacked by a band of Philistines.

"We must go and deliver the place," he announced grimly.

There were now some six hundred men living in the forest of Haret, only a few of whom wanted to go out against the bloodthirsty Philistines. It was bad enough to be sought by King Saul, they said. But to have to deal with still another enemy? This was unnecessary, as well as dangerous. However, David declared that God would give them a speedy victory. There really was no cause for alarm.

Soon these words proved true. David's men easily

defeated the Philistines, and Ceila was saved. But the fruits of peace were short-lived.

"King Saul has heard that we are living in Ceila," a messenger reported one day. "He and his men are on their way now to take us prisoner."

Such news did not surprise David. To capture a constantly moving enemy is a difficult thing. But when that enemy settles in a certain place, particularly in a city, the task becomes much easier.

"King Saul knows this," David told his men. "Hence, I think that we'd better leave Ceila at once."

"But where shall we go, sir?"

"To the desert of Ziph. The king will have a hard time finding us there."

At once a great cheer arose from David's men. What a clever leader they had! The desert of Ziph was a wild and mountainous place, with many deep valleys and caves. In no time at all they could find one or more safe havens.

For several weeks David's followers did elude King Saul. Indeed, it finally seemed as though the king had given up all hope of finding them.

"God is so good!" David declared fervently. "Not only has He preserved me from danger, but my six hundred men as well."

One day, however, there came disturbing news. Eager for a reward, the natives of Ziph had informed King Saul of David's exact whereabouts. Once more the latter was on his way to the desert land of mountains and caves with hundreds of experienced warriors. And this time with the zeal and determination of a man quite sure of his goal.

David did not flinch, however. Instead, he had immediate recourse to prayer. And the prayer which he offered was filled with childlike confidence in the Most High:

Save me, O God, by thy name, and judge me in thy strength.

O God, hear my prayer: give ear to the words of my mouth.

For strangers have risen up against me; and the mighty have sought after my soul: and they have not set God before their eyes.

For behold God is my helper: and the Lord is the protector of my soul.

Turn back the evils upon my enemies; and cut them off in thy truth.

I will freely sacrifice to thee, and will give praise, O God, to thy name: because it is good:

For thou hast delivered me out of all trouble: and my eye hath looked down upon my enemies.*

*Psalm 53

CHAPTER 9

KING SAUL APPROACHES

IN DUE course Saul and his army arrived in the desert. But by now David had fled to a new hiding place near Maon, and the natives of Ziph sought him in vain. Since they knew for certain that there would be no reward unless they delivered David into the king's hand, their anxiety steadily increased.

"Where can he have gone?" they asked one another in angry bewilderment. "And who told him that we were coming to take him prisoner?"

No one could answer these questions, and so the search had to be carried on without direction—accompanied by much grumbling. What a difficult and lonely country was Maon! Why, it was nothing but a wilderness of mountain and rock; of sheer cliffs and deep ravines choked with trees and thick brush! The place also abounded in wild beasts—lions, panthers, bears—not to mention snakes and poisonous insects.

Yet Saul and his men pushed on, and with surprising accuracy. Indeed, the time came when only one mountain peak separated them from David and his little band.

"If we stay here another day, we'll surely be captured, sir," a trembling young shepherd told David one morning. "What are we going to do?"

Seated on the floor of the cave where he had spent the night, the young leader sighed and shook his head wearily.

"Nothing."

"*Nothing?*"

"Haven't you told me that we're surrounded by the king's men? That means there isn't anything we can do—except to die bravely."

"But I don't want to die, sir! I've a wife and family. . ."

"My friend, I don't want to die either."

For a long moment the two outlaws looked silently at each other. A little breeze had sprung up, and now the fearsome sounds of shouting men and clashing armor were clearly audible. Quickly the youthful shepherd fell to his knees.

"Sir, they're just above us—on the other side of the mountain!"

David nodded. "Yes. I know."

"But some of us could escape even now. . .if you'd just give the word. . . ."

David stretched out a gentle hand. "No," he said thoughtfully. "That would be useless." Then, to the astonishment of his terrified companion, he knelt down beside him and began to pray—fervently, earnestly:

I cried to the Lord with my voice: with my voice I made supplication to the Lord.

In his sight I pour out my prayer, and before him I declare my trouble:

When my spirit failed me, then thou knewest my paths.

In this way wherein I walked, they have hidden a snare for me.

I looked on my right hand, and beheld, and there was no one that would know me.

Flight hath failed me: and there is no one that hath regard to my soul.

I cried to thee, O Lord: I said: Thou art my hope, my portion in the land of the living.

Attend to my supplication: for I am brought very low.

Deliver me from my persecutors; for they are stronger than I.

Bring my soul out of prison, that I may praise thy name: the just wait for me, until thou reward me.*

The prayer had a strangely soothing effect upon the young shepherd. Why or how it was he could not say, but fresh strength and courage were suddenly his in abundance.

"Please forgive me for wanting to run away, sir," he whispered humbly. "I . . . I didn't know what I was saying."

David smiled. "I understand," he said.

As the hours passed David offered many other prayers, for never had he been in such a desperate

---

Psalm 141

WITH GREAT CONFIDENCE DAVID BEGAN TO PRAY.

plight as this. As for his followers, scattered about
in various caves, they scarcely dared to breathe.
One false move, and all would be lost. But even as
they huddled in the darkness, awaiting the worst,
hope rose anew in each man's heart. The voices of
the king's soldiers on the other side of the mountain were fading into the distance! And the clatter
of armor was much fainter than before!

"I think that the king is moving camp, sir!"
whispered Abiathar, the son of the high priest,
excitedly. "He's not coming this way after all!"

David grew tense. King Saul leaving? And with
victory just within his grasp? This was unbelievable.
And yet in a little while the report of a breathless
messenger confirmed it. King Saul's forces had
moved down the other side of the mountain and
now were headed for home.

"But why?" cried David incredulously. "What's
happened?"

"The Philistines are marching on Israel, sir!"
gasped the messenger triumphantly. "The king just
received the news, and has gone to do battle with
them!"

Suddenly David fell to his knees. Oh, how good
God was to have heard his prayers! Once again He
had preserved him from danger. Once again He had
delivered him out of the hands of King Saul.

CHAPTER 10

KING SAUL
ENTERS DAVID'S HIDING PLACE

PRESENTLY DAVID and his men left the
wilderness of Maon, thankful indeed for their
new-found liberty. But in the depths of their
hearts they realized that when the war with the
Philistines was over, King Saul would lose no time
in renewing the search for them.

"Fear and jealousy have completely changed the
king," they told one another. "Now he is really a
madman, and will never rest until all of us are
dead."

David agreed, and after some thought decided
that he and his followers should retire to Engaddi
—a desolate place of rocks and caves where possibly they might escape the king's men. The move
proved to be a wise one, for soon messengers
reported that once more King Saul was out to capture David. Even now he was on the way with 3,000
picked warriors.

"What shall we do, sir?" asked David's followers
anxiously. "We're no match at all for a real army."

Confident of God's protection, David issued one simple order. "We'll hide," he said, "high up in the mountains, in the caves of the wild goats."

Soon the six hundred outlaws had settled themselves in the highlands. And at David's suggestion, each man prayed humbly and sincerely for divine assistance.

"The Lord will look after us, providing that we trust in Him completely," David said encouragingly. "After all, what harm have we done?"

Then one day a wave of excitement swept through the hidden encampment. In the distance was the familiar sound of marching men!

"The king is coming, sir!" announced Abiathar, the son of the slain high priest of Nobe. "Look down below!"

Carefully David crept to the mouth of the cave that was now his only home, and scanned the surrounding countryside. Yes, Abiathar was right. Someone had informed King Saul of his victims' move from Maon to Engaddi, and now he had arrived. His banners were plainly visible in the ranks of the foremost soldiers.

"Let no man speak aloud, or stir from his hiding place," David ordered grimly. "If the king glimpses even one of us, we are lost."

This command was faithfully obeyed, and in the days that followed no one spoke above a whisper or made an unnecessary movement. But after a little while there was some restlessness. By now King Saul and his men had disappeared from view— seemingly swallowed up in the vast wilderness of rocks and trees. Surely it was safe to come out from hiding?

David knew better, however. The king's men had not gone home. They had merely broken up into small searching parties.

"The danger is far greater now than before," he declared firmly. "We can hear 100 men climbing over the rocks; perhaps even see them. But five men, or six? Or two or three? Ah, they could easily come upon us with scarcely any warning!"

There was truth in these words, and so the band remained carefully hidden in their caves. But one day David's ever-watchful eyes beheld a startling sight. Directly below his hiding place, not more than 200 yards away, a little group of the enemy was sitting down to rest. Then presently one of them arose and began to clamber up the mountain-side. Slowly he moved from one rock to the next, testing his footing with his spear, then warily pushing on.

"It's the king!" muttered David unbelievingly. *"And heading straight for this cave!"*

With difficulty his followers were restrained from an immediate attack as the solitary figure drew nearer. "No, our ruler is the Lord's anointed one," insisted David. "None of us has the right to touch a hair of his head."

"But sir! He's the cause of all our troubles! Look how cruelly he's treated you!"

David acknowledged this, but nevertheless he ordered his companions to retire to the innermost parts of the cave. "It is not for us to judge anyone," he whispered. "That task is the Lord's."

Grumbling, the men crept back into the shadows. Not even when King Saul stumbled wearily into their hiding place and flung himself down to rest did anyone move. But as the minutes passed and a heavy sleep fell upon him they shifted uneasily. How simple to take a spear and run it through the king's heart! To sever his head with one swift stroke of a sword!

"No," whispered David, reading their thoughts. "Lift not a hand against him."

The men were keenly disappointed. And when David crept forward to cut off the hem of the king's garment—so that later he would be the laughing-stock of the bodyguard waiting below—they could hardly control themselves. What was such a boyish insult in satisfaction for the hardships and persecution which they had endured? Surely their enemy deserved much harsher treatment than this?

However, when the king awoke and started down the mountainside, David was stricken with remorse. A man who came of simple peasant stock had no right even to touch his sovereign, much less to make him an object of scorn.

"My lord!" he called out contritely. "My lord!"

Saul paused, then glanced back fearfully toward the cave. "David!" Is that your voice?"

"Yes, my lord. Oh, why do you persecute me? What harm have I done?"

Then, to the utter amazement of his followers, David began to plead his case. Had he not always been a loyal subject? Had he not always served the

HE WOULD MAKE A LAUGHING-STOCK
OF THE KING!

king faithfully and well? Above all, had he not shown him true mercy a moment ago by refusing to kill him as he slept?

In the relief which followed the shock of fear, Saul remembered some of the affection he had once felt towards David. "My son," he said, "you are more just than I. Oh, David, I know the truth! Someday you will be king. Promise that no harm shall come to my family. . .that you will protect my children and never make them slaves. . ."

Filled for that moment with hope, David generously gave the desired promise. Whereupon the king withdrew, and without another word went down the mountainside with his astonished bodyguard.

Quickly David turned to his companions, his eyes glowing with eagerness. "It was wise to spare him," he declared. "See? Now he must always be in our debt."

But a murmur of indignation ran through the cave. "*Wise*, sir? When he and the others go down the mountain like wild beasts to join the pack?"

"That's right. In a little while they'll be back. What chance then will there be for escape?"

"King Saul will never show us the mercy that you showed him."

"Oh, you should have killed him, sir! Then all our troubles would be over!"

Slowly the glow faded from David's eyes, as the suspicions of his followers recalled past experience to his mind. How, indeed, could the king be trusted when he was really a madman?

"I forgave him because the Lord has forgiven me so many times," he said. "And yet—yes, perhaps we had better find a new hiding place."

However, as the outlaws prepared to leave the cave, David held out a restraining hand. "Let us pray first," he said earnestly. "And let our prayer be of two kinds."

"Two kinds, sir?"

"Yes—for help, and in thanksgiving. For well I know that someday we shall be delivered from all these trials."

Thus, surrounded by his men, David knelt upon the floor of the cave and began to pray:

Have mercy on me, O God, have mercy on me: for my soul trusteth in thee.

And in the shadow of thy wings will I hope, until iniquity pass away.

I will cry to God the most High; to God who hath done good to me.

He hath sent from heaven and delivered me: he hath made them a reproach that trod upon me.

God hath sent his mercy and his truth, and he hath delivered my soul from the midst of the young lions. I slept troubled.

The sons of men, whose teeth are weapons and arrows, and their tongue a sharp sword.

Be thou exalted, O God, above the heavens and thy glory above all the earth.

They prepared a snare for my feet; and they bowed down my soul.

They dug a pit before my face, and they are fallen into it.

My heart is ready, O God, my heart is ready: I will sing, and rehearse a psalm.

Arise, O my glory, arise psaltery and harp: I will arise early.

I will give praise to thee, O Lord, among the people: I will sing a psalm to thee among the nations.

For thy mercy is magnified even to the heavens: and thy truth unto the clouds.

Be thou exalted, O God, above the heavens: and thy glory above all the earth.*

---

*Psalm 56

CHAPTER 11

A SWORD THROUGH DAVID'S HEART

WITHIN A short time the suspicions of David's men were justified. Once more overcome by his insane jealousy, King Saul had ordered his forces to resume the hunt.

"Bring David to me, that I may kill him myself!" he roared. "Never shall he sit upon my throne!"

But although various people sought to betray David into the king's hands, their efforts were in vain. Over mountains, through forests, into deserts, the former shepherd boy led his pursuers with a cunning that amazed everyone.

"He is swifter than the eagle in flight," King Saul's men told one another wearily. "It is impossible to capture him."

"And why is David so wonderfully protected? Because he trusts in the Lord, and praises Him constantly," observed the country folk shrewdly. "Ah, would that he were our king instead of Saul..."

However, there were many times when David's spirits sank to a low ebb, and he found it difficult

to trust in God. How hard to be continually per-
secuted, to have to live like a wild beast in the
wilderness! Then came the day when he could bear
it no longer. He had just had a second chance to
kill King Saul (having come upon him asleep in the
midst of his sleeping followers), but once again he
had been forbearing. He had merely carried away
the king's cup and spear in order to give evidence
of his visit. Yet somehow he could find little consolation in this act of mercy.

"If I spared his life a thousand times, the king
would still hate me," he thought bitterly. "Oh,
what's the use of trying to treat honorably with
him—a madman—any longer?"

Gradually a plan formed in David's mind to
secure peace. He and his men would go to the land
of the Philistines and offer their services to King
Achis. But they would not make the journey fearfully, or in secret, as he himself once had done. No,
they would go openly, and boldly treat with the
king as man to man.

"King Achis already knows that Saul is mad," he
told himself. "He'll understand that we come to
him only to save our lives. Also, that we have something to offer his people, for each of us is skilled
in warfare. After all, haven't we been able to hold
off King Saul's best warriors for several years?"

Achis did receive David warmly, even to the point
of giving him the city of Siceleg for his headquarters. And as the days passed, David proved his
worth as a warrior many times. Over and over again
he went out against the wicked tribes of the

surrounding countryside, capturing their leaders, burning their cities, and otherwise covering himself with glory. Yet in the midst of all these victories, a little voice deep within his heart kept insisting that he should never have hired himself out to the Philistines.

"But why not?" cried David. "Achis is a good man—far better than King Saul. See how well he's treated us since we came to live in his country!"

"Even so, he's a pagan and worships idols," said the little voice. *"It wasn't right to offer him your services."*

"If we'd stayed at home, we might have been dead by now. After all, King Saul and his men. . ."

"Isn't the Lord greater than King Saul? He would have protected you if you'd just left things in His hands."

Reluctantly David acknowledged that he had acted wrongly in hiring himself out to the Philistines. But he made no move to change matters. Indeed, on the day when Achis informed him that he and his men were ready to march against Israel, he readily accepted a place in their ranks. However, shortly before the battle, the Philistine generals discovered his presence and insisted that he be sent home.

"Who can say what this man will do?" they grumbled. "Isn't he an Israelite? Perhaps in the midst of the battle he'll turn against us and go over to King Saul. Then where shall we be?"

Regretfully Achis told David the news. He must return to Siceleg. "But don't worry. I'll send word of how the battle goes," he promised. "Ah, my friend, if only the generals knew you as I do, they'd not be so suspicious."

David smiled. "I understand, Your Majesty. And it's quite all right. Actually your men have good reason to distrust me. I'd do the very same in their place."

Soon David and his followers had returned to Siceleg. But what terrible news greeted them here! During their absence the warlike Amalecites had descended upon the city, captured the women and children as well as all of the flocks, then set fire to the houses and public buildings. Now Siceleg was but a mass of smoldering ruins.

David's heart sank at the dreadful sight. "Already we're being punished for having turned against our own people," he thought fearfully. "Oh, may God forgive us our sin!"

But worse was yet to come. "Sir, we should never have left Siceleg undefended!" declared a number of the fugitives hotly. "Look! Everything's gone from us—wives, children, homes, goods..."

"Yes, and whose fault is it? Why were you so stupid, sir?"

"We owe you obedience no longer!"

"That's right. We'll choose another leader!"

"Down with David!"

"Away with him!"

"Put him to death!"

David looked about in fearful amazement. Never in all their years together had any in his little band dared to criticize him, much less to threaten his

THE CITY WAS A MASS OF SMOLDERING RUINS!

life. But now, desperate at their loss. . .

"Friends, I admit I did wrong," he said falter-
ingly. "I was stupid and careless. But even so, all
is not lost. We can still pursue the Amalecites and
perhaps recover everything. Oh, won't you give me
another chance to be your leader?"

There was a fresh outburst as the outlaws con-
sulted among themselves:

"The Amalecites are too far away by this
time. . ."

"But they can't be! The fires they set here are
still burning."

"They'll have killed our wives and children. . ."

"What? When they can be useful as slaves?"

"But our goods and cattle! They'll surely have
destroyed them. . ."

"No. They'll probably take everything into their
own country."

In the end, David's reasoning prevailed. After
much hesitation and grumbling, his men agreed to
accept him as their leader once more, and to
accompany him in pursuit of the Amalecites. The
decision was a wise one, for before long the enemy
was sighted—feasting and making merry over their
recent victory.

At once a surge of confidence arose throughout
the ranks, and David felt his blood tingle. For he
sensed instantly that the respect and confidence of
his men had been restored to him.

"Advance!" he cried triumphantly. "Don't let a
man escape!"

The Amalecites were so taken by surprise that

within 24 hours they had been utterly defeated. All their ill-gotten goods were restored to the rightful owners, and David returned to Siceleg as a real hero. But his joy did not last for long. Presently a breathless messenger gasped out the news that King Saul had fallen in battle, and three of his sons as well.

"Not Jonathan!" cried David unbelievingly. "Not my good friend!"

The messenger nodded. "Yes, sir. He was among the first to perish."

Suddenly it was as though a sword had pierced David's own heart. Prince Jonathan was dead! His best friend in all the world! His loyal champion! His adopted brother!

"I . . . I can't believe it!" he muttered brokenly. "I can't . . ."

Then, unable to restrain his tears, he fell to his knees and covered his face with his hands, while those standing about listened in awed silence to the words that burst from his heart:

> Hear, O Lord, my prayer: give ear to my supplication in thy truth: hear me in thy justice.
>
> And enter not into judgment with thy servant: for in thy sight no man living shall be justified.
>
> For the enemy hath persecuted my soul: he hath brought down my life to the earth.
>
> He hath made me to dwell in darkness as those that have been dead of old: and my spirit is in anguish within me: my heart within me is troubled.

I remembered the days of old, I meditated on all thy works: I meditated upon the works of thy hands.

I stretched forth my hands to thee: my soul is as earth without water unto thee.

Hear me speedily, O Lord: my spirit hath fainted away.

Turn not away thy face from me, lest I be like unto them that go down into the pit.

Cause me to hear thy mercy in the morning; for in thee have I hoped.

Make the way known to me, wherein I should walk: for I have lifted up my soul to thee.

Deliver me from my enemies, O Lord, to thee have I fled: teach me to do thy will, for thou art my God.

Thy good spirit shall lead me into the right land: for thy name's sake, O Lord, thou wilt quicken me in thy justice.

Thou wilt bring my soul out of trouble: and in thy mercy thou wilt destroy my enemies.

And thou wilt cut off all them that afflict my soul: for I am thy servant.*

Psalm 142

CHAPTER 12

KING DAVID

AVID'S SORROW did not lessen as the weeks passed. What a good friend Jonathan had been! How loyal and generous! Never had there been the slightest misunderstanding between them, although many times Jonathan could have been disturbed at David's popularity, since he himself was King Saul's son and heir.

"How lonely it is without my good brother!" David told himself over and over again. "Oh, dear Lord, what joy is there for me in life now? What work can ever gain hold of my heart?"

The forlorn little prayer was soon answered. In the depths of his soul a heavenly voice spoke consolingly to David, telling him to leave Siceleg and to go to Hebron, a city in the province of Juda. Here he would discover many new and important duties—duties which Jonathan would want him to undertake without delay.

Obediently David set out for Hebron—some 29 miles distant—where he was given a rousing welcome. In fact, from the start the people insisted on making him their king.

"King Saul is dead! Long live King David!" they cried joyfully. "Oh, sire! Your days of wandering are over at last!"

David, who was now thirty years old, was touched at this display of trust and affection, and promised to do his best to be a good ruler. Well he knew that his authority would extend only over the province of Juda, and that in the neighboring provinces there were still some of King Saul's followers who sought his life. But what of this? The Lord would surely protect him as He had always done. All that was necessary was to live one day at a time, and to do that day's work as well as possible.

There was wisdom in this practice, and soon David found himself increasing in strength and worldly goods. Everywhere he went he made new friends, until finally there was not a more powerful man in the whole country.

"Why does the King of Juda prosper at every step?" grumbled the people of the other tribes. "Wasn't he once just a poor shepherd from Bethlehem—with no training at all to be a leader of men?"

"Yes," was the answer, "but the Lord blesses everything that he does because he never begins any work without first asking His help."

It was true. From childhood scarcely a day had passed when David had not knelt to beg God's blessing upon his various undertakings. And the prayer which he offered came from a heart that

knew how to empty itself of selfishness, that was
ready and eager to discover the Will of the
Heavenly Father.

God was so pleased with David's childlike atti-
tude in spiritual matters that He granted him an
extraordinary favor. He allowed him to utter
prayers—or songs—of which He Himself, through
the Holy Spirit, was the Author, and which could
not fail to be pleasing to Him. Sometimes these
prayers were filled with sadness, such as those
offered at the death of Jonathan, or in the midst
of some heavy trial or anxiety. Again, they were
filled with joy and gladness because of the Majesty
of God, at the sight of some beauty in nature, or
in thanksgiving for some great blessing.

Of course David did not fully understand the
wonderful gift which was his. Never once did he
guess that someday the prayers and songs which
Divine Wisdom placed upon his lips—the Psalms—
would be famous all over the world; that men and
women, young and old, would repeat them humbly
and fervently in scores of languages. No, he only
knew that when he emptied his heart of self and
turned to speak to God—in sorrow and contrition,
in joy, in petition, in thanksgiving—beautiful words
were his. They came to him in a mighty flood,
always bringing with them a deep and lasting
peace.

Naturally the people of Juda were proud of their
leader. "There's no greater king than our king,"
they told one another joyfully. "Oh, God be praised
for sending him to us!"

Seven years passed, and David continued to reign wisely and well over Juda. By now, as was the custom for men in high places, he had taken to himself various wives and was the father of six boys. Of all these, he loved his third son, Absalom, the best.

"This is a clever lad," he declared gratefully, "well-built and sturdy. Something tells me that one day he'll make a really fine soldier."

"Yes," agreed his followers. "The young Prince Absalom probably will be a skillful warrior."

But presently David's thoughts turned from planning for the future of his little ones to more pressing matters. Abner, the able general of King Saul's armies, had been murdered—likewise Isboseth, the last remaining son of King Saul. Now the men of Israel, without any capable leader of their own, had sent word to David that they wished him to be their king.

"It's foolish for Juda and the rest of Israel to be enemies any longer," they declared earnestly. "Oh, sire! Forgive us for not paying you homage in the first place! Come and rule over us, and we will be your faithful subjects!"

David knew that the ambassadors from Israel were sincere—partly because their country had declined to such a state that now it was an easy prey for enemy attack, partly because the great majority of the people felt that it was God's Will that David should rule over them.

"Since you wish it, I'll come and be your king," he announced finally. "And I'll do my best to be a good one."

"OH, SIRE, COME, AND RULE OVER US!"

Grateful beyond words, the ambassadors bent low before their new ruler. "May the Lord bless you, sire!" they cried joyfully. "At last peace has come to all of us!"

David meant what he said about being a good king. In fact, he began to pray very earnestly concerning his new duties. And as he prayed, God gave him to understand that as king of both Israel and Juda he must surround himself with trustworthy counsellors—men who were not so much interested in their own welfare as in the welfare of their country. As for himself? Ah, he must continue to lead a good life, always recognizing that his great power over men was but a gift from God.

"Yes, I understand," said David. Then, as had happened so many times before, a new song rose to his lips. The words were uttered by his own tongue, but their inspiration came from Heaven:

Mercy and judgment I will sing to thee, O Lord:
I will sing, and I will understand in the unspotted way, when thou shalt come to me.
I walked in the innocence of my heart, in the midst of my house.
I did not set before my eyes any unjust thing: I hated the workers of iniquities.
The perverse heart did not cleave to me: and the malignant, that turned aside from me, I would not know.
The man that in private detracted his neighbour, him did I persecute.
With him that had a proud eye, and an unsatiable heart, I would not eat.

My eyes were upon the faithful of the earth, to sit with me: the man that walked in the perfect way, he served me.

He that worketh pride shall not dwell in the midst of my house: he that speaketh unjust things did not prosper before my eyes.

In the morning I put to death all the wicked of the land: that I might cut off all the workers of iniquity from the city of the Lord.*

CHAPTER 13

THE ARK OF THE COVENANT

SHORTLY AFTER David had been crowned
King of Israel, he achieved still greater fame
by capturing the city of Jerusalem from the
Jebusites (a pagan race which had been dwelling
there for a long time), and making it his capital.
Splendid new buildings were erected, including a
fine palace, and on all sides Jerusalem became
known as the most important center in the whole
country.

"Just two things are lacking here," David often
told himself. "The Ark of the Covenant, and a magnificent temple in which to shelter it."

The Ark of the Covenant was a wooden box containing the two stone tablets on which were written
the Ten Commandments. Because of the political
unrest of the times, it had been kept for many years
in Cariathiarim, a town a short distance to the
northwest of Jerusalem. But now that peace had
come to all of Israel, David felt justified in remov-
ing the sacred treasure to his own city.

"We must do so with great care and reverence,

however," he decided. "Only a few of the holiest priests will be permitted to touch the Ark."

"Yes," put in his followers. "And wouldn't it be well to have a great procession, sire? With music and singing, and all the leaders of our provinces taking part?"

David agreed that the transfer of the Ark of the Covenant from Cariathiarim to Jerusalem ought to be conducted with great splendor. After all, the stone tablets containing the Ten Commandments were the holiest possession of the Israelites. Some 400 years ago they had been given to Moses by God Himself. It was impossible to pay them sufficient honor.

"Yes, we'll have a real celebration," he promised, "the greatest that anyone has ever seen."

Soon word had gone about that the Ark of the Covenant was to be brought to Jerusalem, the city of David. On the day appointed, 30,000 men assembled in Cariathiarim from all parts of the kingdom, together with their wives and children. The streets were decorated with rich hangings; the people wore their finest clothes, and young and old carried a variety of musical instruments— flutes, harps, trumpets, cymbals and tambourines —on which they were to play the sacred songs of Israel.

At the sight of the vast and eager throng, the gay flags and fluttering banners, David's heart filled with joy. What a glorious day this was! And how wonderful that the Ark of the Covenant was about to enter the city of Jerusalem—*his* city! From now on the place would be the religious center of Israel, as well as the political one.

"Dear Lord, thank You for this great honor," he whispered. "And please help us to be worthy of it..."

Presently the enormous procession got underway, with David at the head playing upon his harp in a real ecstasy of joy. Behind him, 30,000 voices raised themselves in song—such a thundering chorus of praise that the very earth seemed to tremble with the glory of it all—the triumphant notes of the trumpets, the clash of cymbals and tambourines, the soaring tones of the flutes and harps:

> O kingdoms of the earth, sing ye unto God, make melody to the Lord, who is borne through the heavens, the heavens of old!

But alas! As the mighty cavalcade neared the gates of Jerusalem and the people made ready to sing still another song which David had written, there was a sudden cry of horror. Oza, one of the men in the rear of the procession, had been struck dead!

"We were at a rough place in the road, and Oza tried to keep the Ark from falling!" gasped out the terrified messengers who brought David the horrifying news.

"That's right. The oxen were beginning to kick, and the cart bearing the Ark was almost tipping over..."

"Yes, and Oza stretched out his hand to save the Ark..."

"He was in charge, but for a moment he forgot that only the priests may touch it..."

"As soon as he did touch it, it was as though lightning had struck him!"

"He fell dead at once!"

"Yes. And now the people are in a dreadful panic, sire. Oh, what are we going to do?"

David was aghast. Instead of giving glory to God by a great procession, he and his followers had given serious offense. Oza's action in striving to save the Ark from harm might seem a perfectly natural and innocent one—indeed, the only one possible under the circumstances—but there were other things to consider. For instance, why had he permitted the sacred treasure to be put in an ox-drawn cart in the first place? Why had he not arranged for the priests to place it upon the shoulders of their assistants, so that it might be *carried* into Jerusalem? For generations this had been the only accepted mode of travel for the precious relic.

Suddenly fear filled David's soul. Pale and trembling, he gave orders that the procession must disband at once. The people were to return to their homes, humbly begging God's mercy for the terrible offense which had been committed. As for the Ark itself? The priests were to carry it without delay into the nearest house and leave it there—with all due reverence and ceremony.

That night Jerusalem was shrouded in gloom. Would God punish His people still further for their lack of respect concerning His Commandments? Would some terrible calamity occur—an earthquake, a famine, a fearful pestilence?

"Spare us, O Lord!" cried David humbly. "Forgive us our sin against Your holy law. . ."

"Spare us, O Lord!" repeated the people fearfully. "Have mercy upon Your erring children. . ."

God was touched by such contrite prayer, and He withheld further punishment. Indeed, when three months had passed, He inspired David to bring the Ark into Jerusalem—but this time upon the shoulders of qualified men, not in a cart drawn by oxen.

"The house where the Ark has been resting these last three months has prospered wonderfully," David declared. "Oh, how wonderful if our city should also be blessed by the presence of God's holy law!"

Soon a second procession had been arranged, even more magnificent than the first. Once again the people assembled. Once again colorful flags and banners fluttered in the breeze, with the air echoing to the sound of trumpets, cymbals and flutes, and to thousands of voices raised in triumphant song:

> The earth is the Lord's and the fulness thereof: the world, and all they that dwell therein.
>
> For he hath founded it upon the seas; and hath prepared it upon the rivers.
>
> Who shall ascend into the mountain of the Lord: or who shall stand in his holy place?
>
> The innocent in hands, and clean of heart, who

hath not taken his soul in vain, nor sworn deceit-
fully to his neighbour.

He shall receive a blessing from the Lord, and
mercy from God his Saviour.

This is the generation of them that seek him,
of them that seek the face of the God of Jacob.*

David was so carried out of himself at the splendor of the great occasion that suddenly he laid
aside his royal dignity. Harp in hand, he began to
dance for pure joy! Yet as the Ark neared the tabernacle or dwelling which had been prepared for it,
his happiness increased still further. By now the triumphant music had reached its thrilling climax,
with singers and musicians demanding that the
keepers of the tabernacle give immediate entrance
to the King of glory:

Lift up your gates, O ye princes, and be ye lifted
up, O eternal gates: and the King of Glory shall
enter in.

Who is this King of Glory? the Lord who is
strong and mighty: the Lord mighty in battle.

Lift up your gates, O ye princes, and be ye lifted
up, O eternal gates: and the King of Glory shall
enter in.

Who is this King of Glory? the Lord of hosts,
he is the King of Glory.*

As the strains of the glorious music finally died
away, a solemn hush fell upon the waiting throng.
Then the doors of the tabernacle swung wide.

---

*Psalm 23

THE BEARERS OF THE ARK
MOVED SLOWLY FORWARD.

Slowly, reverently, the bearers of the Ark moved forward with their sacred burden.

David's eyes shone. What a wonderful day this was! And how good of God to permit His holy law to rest among them!

CHAPTER 14

DAVID FALLS INTO SIN

THE PRESENCE of the Ark of the Covenant in Jerusalem was a source of great consolation to David. Of course the Lord was everywhere, but how much closer He seemed now! The two stone tablets within the Ark had been His special gift to the Israelites. By obeying the Ten Commandments written upon them, a man or woman could be sure of leading a good life.

Yet there was still something lacking to David's happiness. "If we just had a real temple here in which to put the Ark!" he often thought. "It doesn't seem right that I should live in a fine palace when the Word of God rests in a poor and humble dwelling. . . ."

Presently he discussed the matter with the holy prophet Nathan (his religious counsellor), and the latter agreed that Jerusalem ought to have a temple. What if skilled workmen and fine materials were lacking? They could easily be brought in from the nearby city of Tyre—as had been done in the case of David's own palace. However, a little later

Nathan decided otherwise. He had prayed long and earnestly about the matter, and now God had given him to understand that it was not the former shepherd boy of Bethlehem who was to build the temple of Jerusalem. It was the son who would succeed to his throne.

David received this decree calmly. Who was he to question the Divine Will? It was an honor sufficiently great that the building of the temple should be reserved for any one of his family.

"Behold the servant of the Most High," he replied humbly. "May His Will be done in all things!"

Of course God was pleased with such humility, as well as with the splendid way in which David was governing his people, and as the years passed He sent him many blessings. Indeed, Israel defeated every enemy that came against it—the Philistines, the Moabites, the Syrians, the Ammonites—until finally there was not a stronger or a richer nation.

"How far away all my troubles seem now!" David thought gratefully. "It's hard to believe that I was ever in danger of being murdered by King Saul... that I had to spend years of my life hiding from him in lonely caves...."

The Devil, however, was far from being happy over David's good fortune. *"The King of Israel serves God too faithfully,"* he grumbled. *"He's always making up songs in His honor, and doing good to this one and that. If this keeps up, I'll never be able to win his soul."*

The other devils agreed. King David was the only just and prayerful ruler for miles around. Unless he could be led into serious sin, he would become a saint and so go to Heaven when he died. And who could tell when death might come? Why, the king was now more than 50 years old. God might see fit to call him at any moment.

"*We've wasted enough time,*" the devils decided. "*We ought to get busy at once about winning the king's soul.*"

"*Yes, but how?*"

"*Why, we'll get him to commit a lot of little sins.*"

"*Little sins? They won't send him to Hell.*"

"*No, but they'll get him ready for the ones that will.*"

"*That's right. King David is just like any other man. When he becomes used to little sins, he'll fall into the big ones without too much trouble.*"

"*Yes, and once he's committed one big sin . . .*"

"*It'll be fairly easy to get him to fall into a second.*"

"*And a third.*"

"*And a fourth.*"

"*And then he'll be ours! He'll forget about God and never be able to go to Heaven!*"

David never suspected the evil plot which the devils were hatching. In fact, since he had been leading a good life for years, grace was strong within him and he succeeded in overcoming the smaller temptations which they now began to send his way—the chance to lie, to cheat, to be unkind, to shirk this or that duty. As for the big sins which they suggested, he turned aside from them in horror. How could a man even dream of committing such vile and filthy crimes? It was impossible.

Of course all Hell was furious that David was escaping their clutches. *"We've made a big mistake,"* was the general opinion. *"David is a holy man, and he sees the ugliness of sin more clearly than most people. We'll have to try some other plan with him."*

"All right. But what?"

"Well, the king is a poet and a musician. He likes nice things."

"And we've been tempting him with ugly things?"

"Yes. Now we must make sin seem attractive, even beautiful."

"Beautiful!"

"That's right. We must get him to desire something, good and beautiful in itself, that isn't his. We must make him think that he can't be happy without it. Then the first thing we know—holy man though he is—he'll be ready to steal, even to commit murder, in order to have it."

As King of Israel, David had everything that anyone could want—wealth, power, friends, the trust and affection of his people. According to custom, he also had several wives. But on the day when the devils began to put their new plan into effect, the great blessings that had made him so happy suddenly lost much of their sweetness. His discontent grew day by day, and soon all that he possessed had become less in his eyes than dust and ashes. At last there was only one thing in all the world that seemed good and desirable to David. This was the love of Bethsabee, an attractive young woman who lived in Jerusalem.

"If I could just have her for my wife, I'd be the happiest man in all Israel," he told himself. "I'd never want for anything else."

"*But Bethsabee is already married*," warned a little voice in his heart. "*Her husband Urias is one of the bravest men in your army.*"

David shifted uneasily. "There's probably a way out of that difficulty."

"*There's no way out. And you know it.*"

"But if I think hard . . ."

"*What? You're going to think hard about breaking one of God's Commandments?*"

Reluctantly David was compelled to acknowledge honestly that he could not marry the wife of another man and still remain the friend of God. But as the days passed, the temptation to steal Bethsabee grew ever stronger and finally he took her to live with him—secretly. Then, to the delight of all the devils, a plan formed in his mind whereby he might gain public and lawful possession of Bethsabee. He would give orders for her husband Urias to be put in the front line of the battle that just then was being waged against the Ammonites. There could be little doubt that the unfortunate man would soon fall a victim to the enemy, and then Bethsabee would be free to marry. . . .

Of course no one knew of David's evil scheme. And when Urias was killed by the Ammonites and the king took Bethsabee for his wife (after a suitable period of mourning), no one suspected anything. But God knew all that had happened and was exceedingly angry with the man who up until now had been His faithful servant.

"Speak to David, and tell him that because he has sinned against Me, he must be punished," He told the holy prophet Nathan. "Tell him that because he has broken My Commandments, sorrow of all kinds shall come upon him and his whole house."

Nathan, astonished and grieved, lost no time in reproving the king for his sins. And as he delivered God's terrifying message, a sudden and terrible sorrow filled David's heart.

"I *have* been wicked!" he moaned. "Dreadfully wicked! I deserve to go to Hell a thousand times. . ."

Then as he considered God's boundless kindness—how He had made him, an ignorant shepherd, the head of a great kingdom, how He had preserved his life on countless occasions and given him all that a man could desire—he hid his face in his hands and burst into tears. A small sin was a serious offense against so good a God. How much more the dreadful crimes of taking another man's wife for his own and then causing the innocent man to be slain?

Nathan, startled at the intensity of David's grief, tried to speak consolingly of God's mercy to even the greatest of sinners. But David scarcely heard him. Heedless of his royal dignity, conscious only that he had grievously offended the heavenly Father, he had fallen to his knees and now was pouring out his soul in an agony of sorrow:

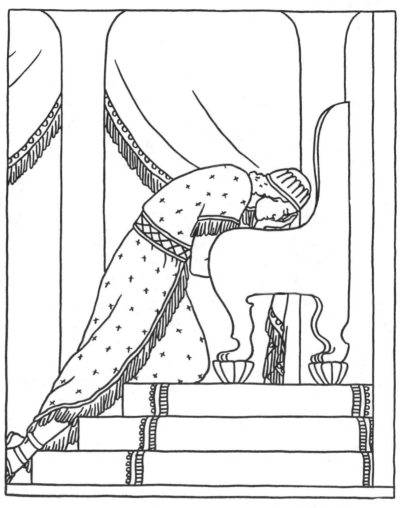

"I'VE BEEN DREADFULLY WICKED!"

Have mercy on me, O God, according to thy mercy.

And according to the multitude of thy tender mercies blot out my iniquity.

Wash me yet more from my iniquity, and cleanse me from my sin.

For I know my iniquity, and my sin is always before me.

To thee only have I sinned, and have done evil before thee: that thou mayst be justified in thy words, and mayst overcome when thou art judged.

For behold I was conceived in iniquities; and in sins did my mother conceive me.

For behold thou hast loved truth: the uncertain and hidden things of thy wisdom thou hast made manifest to me.

Thou shalt sprinkle me with hyssop, and I shall be cleansed: thou shalt wash me, and I shall be made whiter than snow.

To my hearing thou shalt give joy and gladness: and the bones that have been humbled shall rejoice.

Turn away thy face from my sins, and blot out all my iniquities.

Create a clean heart in me, O God: and renew a right spirit within my bowels.

Cast me not away from thy face; and take not thy holy spirit from me.

Restore unto me the joy of thy salvation, and strengthen me with a perfect spirit.

I will teach the unjust thy ways: and the wicked shall be converted to thee.

Deliver me from blood, O God, thou God of my salvation: and my tongue shall extol thy justice.

O Lord, thou wilt open my lips: and my mouth shall declare thy praise.

For if thou hadst desired sacrifice, I would indeed have given it: with burnt offerings thou wilt not be delighted.

A sacrifice to God is an afflicted spirit: a contrite and humbled heart, O God, thou wilt not despise.*

*Psalm 50

CHAPTER 15

TERRIBLE NEWS

GOD HEARD David's heartfelt prayer and forgave him his sins. But David still had to be punished. Soon the prophecies uttered by Nathan began to come true. Trouble of all kinds descended upon the royal household. A crisis was reached when a quarrel between Amnon, David's first-born son, and Absalom, his third, ended in the murder of Amnon by Absalom.

David was heartbroken, especially when he discovered that Absalom had fled for refuge to distant Gessur. "In my old age my children act like pagans and scandalize the people!" he cried despairingly. "Oh, how can I bear it?"

The prophet Nathan held him in a stern gaze. "Isn't this part of the punishment due the evil in your own life?" he suggested quietly. "Be wise. Bear it patiently."

"But a son of mine has murdered his brother! Surely that's too much for any man to bear!"

Nathan hesitated, then pointed an accusing finger. "Have you forgotten the Lord's words after your own sin? *'The sword shall never depart from your house, because you have despised Me. . . Behold, I will raise up evil against you out of your own house. . . .'* "

David bowed his head. Of course he had not forgotten the terrible words which God had spoken through the mouth of His holy prophet. How could he, when already the bitter fruit of his sinfulness was seen in the death of one son and the flight into exile of another?

"But Absalom left without a word for me," he murmured brokenly. "The light of my life. . .the most promising of all my sons. . ."

"Your son was the murderer of his brother!"

"I would have forgiven him if he had just come to me trustingly. . .as a child should come to his father, no matter what his crime. . . ."

"Bear this trial in patience also," Nathan commanded. "Remember, it is the Will of the Lord which sends it to you."

Humbly David consented, and for three years he strove to blot out from his mind the thought of the son whom he loved so dearly. But finally it was decided that Absalom might return from exile. Of course, if public scandal were to be avoided he could not be reinstated in the king's good graces at once. He must live quietly in Jerusalem for some two years before he could even be admitted to his father's presence. But then, all being well, the remembrance of his crime would have died away, and he could gradually resume his rightful place in society.

How happy David was on that day when Absalom finally stood before him in the royal palace! "The sun shines again after an eternity of darkness!" he exclaimed joyfully. "Ah, Absalom, my son! Welcome home!"

Absalom, who was an extremely handsome young man in his middle twenties, was shrewd enough to realize that despite his grievous crime he was still his father's favorite son. As a child he had taken advantage of this fact many times, trusting to his ready wit and charm of manner to preserve him from reproach for his various misdeeds. But now it must be different. The easy ways were to be set aside, the careless acceptance of the royal favor. Even as the lowliest servant might have done, he would prostrate himself at the king's feet.

"Father, forgive me for all the grief that I've caused you," he whispered penitently. "I . . . I've been very wicked."

Tears of sympathy sprang to David's eyes. Here was a good youth—impulsive, headstrong, quick to anger, yes—yet equally quick to admit his short-comings and to sorrow for them. . . .

"Rise, my son, rise!" he cried. "All is forgiven!" And hastening forward, he helped the prodigal to his feet and embraced him warmly.

Alas! Much grief was in store for David, who never dreamed that Absalom was far from being sorry for having murdered his brother, or grateful for being allowed to return home. Indeed, in the depths of his heart the young man nourished an extremely bitter grudge for the way he had been treated by family and by friends.

"My brother Amnon was a wretch and a beast,"
he told himself, even as he returned David's affec-
tionate embraces. "He committed dreadful sins
against God and man. But did my father ever punish him, as was his duty? Did he ever so much as
speak one reproving word? Of course not! He was
too weak and fearful—*and lazy!*"

The days passed, and the more Absalom brooded
over the sins of his dead brother, the angrier he
became with the father who had permitted such
wickedness to go unchecked. Of course he himself
should not have taken the law into his own hands
and ordered his servants to kill the wretched
Amnon. Such punishment should have been left to
God. But to have to spend three years in exile for
this deed, then stay in retirement another two years
before his family would have anything to do with
him. . . .

"Five years of my life wasted!" he fumed. "And
only because I did what any real man would feel
like doing! But Father will pay for his injustice.
Never fear."

Poor David! He never suspected the presence of
this bitterness in his son's soul, nor the evil plot
against him which was taking form in the young
man's mind. In fact, he knew only a righteous pride
and joy that Absalom was home again. Ah, how
handsome the boy was! How expert with a sword,
a spear, a bow and arrow! And how popular with
young and old! Every morning, heedless of his per-
sonal comfort, he was to be found at the city gates,

mixing freely with all classes and doing what he could for those in want.

"Prince Absalom calls every man his brother," declared one of David's counsellors admiringly. "There's no better-liked young man in all Jerusalem."

"That's right," put in another. "He especially goes out of his way to help all strangers within our city. There's nothing that he won't do for them."

"As for the sick and poor—they've never had such a good friend," insisted a third.

David's eyes shone with satisfaction. "May the Lord be blessed for giving me such a dutiful son," he said gratefully.

Then one day came terrible and unexpected news. In the city of Hebron, David's former capital, Absalom had risen up against his father and proclaimed himself king of all Israel! Dazzled by his winning ways and fair promises, thousands were siding with him in his rebellion. David had reigned long enough, they said. It was time for a younger man to take charge of the country.

"It means war, sire!" gasped out a terrified messenger. "All Israel is following after Absalom!"

"That's right!" cried a breathless companion. "Even now a real army is marching on Jerusalem!"

Stunned and heartsick, David brought himself to the full realization of the dreadful report. Absalom, the most beloved of all his sons, had revolted against his authority! His soldiers were less than thirty miles away, prepared to fall upon Jerusalem with fire and sword if it did not yield to them immediately. . . .

"Where is Achitophel, my chief counsellor?" he cried desperately. "Surely he had some inkling of all this trouble. Why didn't he warn me?"

The messengers looked at each other hesitantly. "Achitophel isn't here, sire."

"Well, where is he?"

"In Hebron."

"In Hebron?"

"Yes. Oh, sire! Achitophel is now chief counsellor to your son!"

With a great groan David hid his face in his hands. Achitophel, the most able statesman at court, had gone over to Absalom's side! Oh, what dreadful news! And yet, how much more dreadful to realize that this trusted friend had been a traitor for months—perhaps even for years—since a rebellion such as Absalom had produced could not have been effected overnight. It was the fruit of much careful thought and planning.

There was no time for idle grief, however, and soon David had made up his mind. Accepting the present tragedy as a further, just punishment for his sins, he declared that he would not do battle with Absalom. Why should innocent men be slain, and a beautiful city laid waste, to the end that an aging ruler might retain his throne?

"Let my son wear the crown if he wishes," he sighed wearily. "It will weigh more heavily than he thinks."

"But you can't stay here in the palace, sire!" cried the court officials. "You must flee to some safe place! And at once! Why, even now Prince

Absalom is on the way. . . ."

A bitter smile curved David's lips. From boyhood he had been in danger of his life many times—in battles with the Philistines, at the hands of King Saul, in encounters with the Amalecites, the Moabites, the Syrians, the Ammonites. With God's help, he had always emerged victorious. But now. . .oh, could it be that he was to die at the hands of his own people? *And led by his own son?*

Suddenly a new thought concerning the situation came to David with the swiftness of shock. Absalom must be prevented from committing the terrible sin of killing his own father!

"My friends, you're right!" he said sharply. "It *is* best to leave the city. Perhaps we can find safety in the country along the Jordan, where the tribes have always been friendly. . . ."

"Yes, sire!" cried the officials in relief. "Come— we'll help you to get ready."

In just a little while the people of Jerusalem witnessed a moving sight. David and the faithful members of his household, barefoot and clothed in poor garments, were filing out of the palace gates. All had their heads shrouded, as befitted mourners, and a number were weeping bitterly.

"Look! The king can barely walk for his grief!" whispered a young woman. "Oh, may God have mercy on him!"

Her husband shook his head. "I've never seen him look so old and feeble before," he muttered. "Ah, it's not easy for a father to have a son turn against him. . . ."

"LOOK! THE KING CAN BARELY WALK
FOR HIS GRIEF!"

A wave of compassion arose among the people in the streets, and there were earnest declarations of loyalty and allegiance. But David, his head bowed, his heart numb with sorrow, was scarcely aware of what was said. Other words were ringing in his ears now—holy words, words of prayer—inspired by God Himself:

Why, O Lord, are they multiplied that afflict me? many are they who rise up against me.

Many say to my soul: There is no salvation for him in his God.

But thou, O Lord, art my protector, my glory, and the lifter up of my head.

I have cried to the Lord with my voice: and he hath heard me from his holy hill.

I have slept and have taken my rest: and I have risen up, because the Lord hath protected me.

I will not fear thousands of the people, surrounding me: arise, O Lord; save me, O my God.

For thou hast struck all them who are my adversaries without cause: thou hast broken the teeth of sinners.

Salvation is of the Lord: and thy blessing is upon thy people.*

*Psalm 3

CHAPTER 16

DAVID FLEES JERUSALEM

A S DAVID made his way out of the city, he
met grieving friends who begged permission
to accompany him. Two of these, the high
priests Sadoc and Abiathar, with their attendants,
had even gone so far as to bring with them the Ark
of the Covenant. If King David was to live in exile,
they said, it was only right that he should know the
strengthening presence of Israel's sacred treasure.
A new tabernacle or dwelling place could be made
for it, and every day the king could comfort himself
by going within to pray. . . .

But David shook his head. "No," he murmured,
"carry the Ark back into the city. If I find grace
in the sight of the Lord, He will bring me to Jerusalem again, and will show it to me."

Reluctantly the high priests returned to Jerusalem with their holy burden, and David continued
on his way. But he had progressed only as far as
the summit of Mount Olivet—a wooded hill outside
the city—when he saw still another sorrowing
friend hastening toward him. This was Chusai, an

able and experienced statesman, who announced that he, too, was going into exile with David.

"I could never serve a false king, even though he were your son, sire," he declared earnestly. "Oh, what a sad day for Israel when the Lord's anointed is driven from his throne!"

David, his heart heavy with grief, thanked Chusai for his willingness to follow him into exile, but he begged him to render another kind of service. Would he return at once to Jerusalem? Then, when Absalom arrived, would he hurry to the palace and offer his allegiance? Most important of all, would he make a great show of eager joy over the arrival of the young prince?

"*Eager joy?* But sire! How can I?"

David gently stretched out his hand. "My friend, I know what you are thinking," he said wearily. "But have you forgotten that Achitophel, one of the wisest men in my kingdom, has gone over to Absalom's side?"

Chusai hesitated. "You mean..."

"I mean, if *you* win Absalom's confidence, my kingdom can be saved."

"But sire..."

"You, too, are known to be a wise man, Chusai. Ah, suppose you were to sit at the king's council table...and by cunning should cause each of Achitophel's recommendations to be overruled... while yet remaining friendly with Absalom...and then sent word to me by trusted messenger of everything that took place...wouldn't such service be beyond all worth?"

Chusai bowed low. "My lord, you have spoken," he murmured. "I have only to obey."

"Then you will go back to the city? You will do your best to win my son's confidence and to outwit Achitophel?"

"I will do my best."

David looked affectionately upon this old and trusted friend, so ready to change all his plans and assume a perilous mission, the failure of which could mean only one thing—death!

"May the Lord bless you, Chusai," he said earnestly, "now and forever."

The two parted then—Chusai for Jerusalem, where by now many of the people were in a panic, not knowing whether to follow David into exile or to cast their lot with Absalom—David for the safety of the country along the Jordan.

The hours passed, and after partaking of some refreshment, the king and his company—barefoot, their heads still shrouded in the fashion of mourners—moved down the other side of Mount Olivet. And as he walked, it seemed to the penitent king that his whole lifetime of 62 years was now opening out before him in a series of dream pictures. Here he was a child again, watching his father's flocks in the fields outside Bethlehem. Here he was a teen-age boy, challenging Goliath to single combat. Again, he was a young man in his twenties, seated at the feet of King Saul and striving to cheer him with a lively tune. Still again, he was with his good friend Jonathan. . . .

Suddenly a stream of curses filled the air, and

"YOU MAN OF BLOOD!" CRIED SEMEI FURIOUSLY.

the dream pictures dissolved. "You man of blood!" screamed a harsh and horrible voice. "The Lord has repaid you for all the blood of the house of Saul! Because you have usurped the kingdom in his stead, the Lord has given the kingdom into the hand of Absalom your son!"

David looked up in astonishment. A man whose eyes glittered with rage was standing by the roadside, cursing and flinging stones and dirt upon him and his passing company. This unheard-of disrespect was too much for some of the royal bodyguard, particularly for Abisai, David's nephew, who begged permission to go at once and put the man to death. But David shook his head.

"Let him alone, and let him curse."

"But this wretch is one of Saul's kinsmen, sire! He has never forgotten that your family, not his, is the reigning one in Israel. See? He would kill you if he could."

"If my own son seeks my life, how much the more should this poor creature? Let him alone that he may curse as the Lord has bidden him."

"The Lord, sire?"

"Yes. For it is He Who has sent this trial. If I bear it patiently, perhaps He may look upon my affliction and render me good for the cursing of this day."

Reluctantly David's soldiers sheathed their swords, but they continued to walk several ranks deep on either side of their sovereign. At least they would give him some protection against the stones and dirt which his enemy—whose name they had discovered to be Semei—was hurling upon him.

But even with this, Abisai was far from being satisfied. "Would that I might kill this Semei of the house of Saul," he muttered.

Joab, his brother, clenched his fists. "I, too," he murmured. "But keep such thoughts to yourself. These days the king has only one aim: to bear all hardship in atonement for his sins."

It was true. Since the day when the prophet Nathan had told David of the Lord's anger against him for having taken Bethsabee to live with him while she was still the wife of another, then contrived the death of her husband, he had mourned over his sinfulness. And though Bethsabee was now legally his wife and the mother of the boy Solomon, who one day would succeed to the throne of Israel and build the glorious temple of Jerusalem, David's sorrow over his crimes had not decreased. In fact, he had gradually come to recognize in each disappointment which came his way, each pain and heartache, a heaven-sent means for satisfying God's justice.

There were many pains and heartaches for David during the next few days as he began his exile in the country along the Jordan. Oh, how he missed his beautiful city of Jerusalem, and the opportunity to spend a while in prayer before the Ark of the Covenant! From time to time he would give voice to these longings in song, comparing his desire to kneel once more in God's holy place to that of a desert yearning for rain:

O God, my God, to thee do I watch at break of day.

For thee my soul hath thirsted; for thee my flesh, O how many ways!

In a desert land, and where there is no way, and no water: so in the sanctuary have I come before thee, to see thy power and thy glory.

For thy mercy is better than lives: thee my lips shall praise.

Thus will I bless thee *all* my life long: and in thy name I will lift up my hands.

Let my soul be filled as with marrow and fatness: and my mouth shall praise thee with joyful lips.

If I have remembered thee upon my bed, I will meditate on thee in the morning: because thou hast been my helper.

And I will rejoice under the covert of thy wings: my soul hath stuck close to thee: thy right hand hath received me.

But they have sought my soul in vain, they shall go into the lower parts of the earth:

They shall be delivered into the hands of the sword, they shall be the portions of foxes.

But the king shall rejoice in God, all they shall be praised that swear by him: because the mouth is stopped of them that speak wicked things.*

Then suddenly word arrived from Jerusalem. By a stroke of good luck Chusai had been able to win the confidence of Absalom and to defeat the move of crafty Achitophel, who had recommended that

*Psalm 62

David should be pursued at once. Much valuable time had thus been gained for David, but now he must use it to advantage by crossing the Jordan without delay and withdrawing into safer country.

"War must come, sire," warned Chusai in his message, "and I beg you to prepare for the worst. Prince Absalom is not content that you have fled from Jerusalem. He seeks your very life. In a few days he will be ready to march against you with thousands of soldiers."

Sick at heart, David gave the word for his followers to cross the Jordan and to proceed to Mahanaim, a town some thirty-seven miles away in the province of Galaad. It would take several days at least for Absalom and his forces to reach here. In the meantime, plans could be made for the inevitable battle.

But scarcely had they pitched camp at Mahanaim when David's men insisted that he was not well enough to go out to battle with them. The sorrow and strain of the last few weeks had been exhausting for a man of his age. Besides, the presence of the king amidst his men would incur tremendous risks. The enemy would consider the slaying or capture of the leader as equal to the destruction of 10,000 men, and would certainly concentrate the fury of their attack upon this objective. Surely it would be best for the king to remain within the city? The knowledge that he was alive and safe here would be all the inspiration his own followers would need.

David did not argue, knowing full well his weakness and fatigue. He knew, too, that he could place entire confidence in the leadership of three of the ablest warriors to be found anywhere—Joab, Abisai and Ethai. But there was one desire of his which he well knew they would not anticipate. On the morning when the troops set out from Mahanaim for Ephraim Forest—where, according to reliable reports, Absalom and his followers had now assembled—he came to the city gates to make a request which amazed the three generals.

"Spare the young Prince Absalom!" he begged earnestly, unshed tears glistening in his eyes. "If you should come upon him in the midst of the battle, merely take him prisoner and bring him to me."

Joab, Abisai and Ethai looked at one another. Spare the young Prince Absalom? Not silence that proud and treacherous tongue at the first opportunity?

"Save me the boy Absalom!" David pleaded, noting the stern and darkening faces of his three chieftains. "Save me my little lad...."

There was a moment's silence. Then slowly Joab, Abisai and Ethai bowed their heads. No harm should come to the young prince, they promised. Although he was a traitor, even though thousands of innocent men were about to die in battle because of him, they would be merciful, since the king his father commanded it.

CHAPTER 17

DAVID LEARNS HUMILITY

A LL DAY David sat by the city gates, waiting for news of the battle which he knew must now be raging in Ephraim Forest. At last a messenger arrived with the longed-for word. The king's troops had been victorious! There had been a great slaughter of Absalom's men, so that now at least 20,000 of them lay dead upon the battlefield, and several thousand more were in panic-stricken retreat. . . .

"But the young prince himself—is he safe?" cried David anxiously. "Has he been taken prisoner as I ordered and brought to me here?"

The messenger hesitated. "I left the headquarters of Joab with only one piece of news, sire. About the victory."

David hid his disappointment as best he could, motioned to the messenger to pass into the city for some well-earned food and rest, then resumed his stand at the gates—pacing restlessly up and down as he waited for further word from the battlefield. This was not long in coming, for even as the first

111

messenger made his way into the city, a second
arrived at the gates. He also was breathless and
eager, exclaiming in an excited jumble over the skill
and bravery of Joab, Abisai and Ethai in routing the
enemy so quickly.

"Yes! Yes!" cried David impatiently. "But what
of Absalom? What about my boy?"

The messenger took a deep breath, glanced
briefly at his sovereign, then lowered his eyes. "Let
the enemies of my lord the king, and all that rise
against him unto evil, be as the young man is," he
said slowly.

David paled. "Y-you mean..."

"I mean that Absalom is dead, sire."

"Oh, no!"

"Yes, sire. In the midst of Ephraim Forest."

For a moment David stood as if in a trance. Then
he staggered back against the gates, his face hidden
in his hands. "My son Absalom, Absalom my son!"
he cried sorrowfully. "Would to God that I might
die for you, Absalom my son! My son Absalom!"

Those watching the tragic scene were deeply
touched, and hastened to offer the king comfort in
his sorrow. But David withdrew at once and shut
himself away in a small room in the watchtower
above the city gates, refusing to eat or drink.
Indeed, when but an hour had passed, it was
rumored among his followers that the king was
about to go mad from grief.

"Listen!" they whispered fearfully, as over and
over again the agonizing cry arose from the small
room above the city gates:

"My son Absalom, Absalom my son! Would to God that I might die for you, Absalom my son, my son Absalom!"

By nightfall, far from being the center of merry-making and feasting which one might have expected after a great military victory, Mahanaim was a place of deep gloom. How could anyone think of giving the returning soldiers the rousing welcome which they deserved when King David had shut himself away to bewail his son's death? Yet here and there in the darkened streets, men and women did gather in cautious groups to hear the story of the day's great events:

"Absalom's men were overcome before they even knew what was happening...."

"That's right. His generals were no match for ours...."

"When the young prince found that out, he tried to run away...."

"Yes. He rode his mule at top speed right into the depths of the forest...."

"But the animal was terrified, and passed too close to a low-hanging oak...."

"And Absalom's head caught in the branches...."

"Then when the mule ran on, he was left hanging there...."

"An easy target for any man's spear...."

"Only no man dared to kill him, because of the king's order...."

"No man except Joab."

"That's right. No man except Joab."

It was true. Absalom had not actually died in battle, but from the lances which Joab ran through his heart as he struggled to free himself from the branches of the oak. (The old warrior had dared to defy the king's order because he felt that Israel could never know peace as long as the treacherous Absalom remained alive.)

David was more heartbroken than ever when he learned the true story of his son's death. Nevertheless, he managed to accept even this tragedy in a truly admirable spirit. It, too, he acknowledged, was part of the punishment due his sins. So also were the other hardships and trials which had come his way since he had been triumphantly escorted back to Jerusalem by his people—a rebellion led by a man named Seba, a famine of three years, and four separate encounters with the Philistines.

For a time, after the tragic death of Absalom, this spirit of resignation allowed David to live in peace. And then a dreadful temptation overtook him. Again he fell into scandalously serious sin! Not that he again stole another man's wife or caused innocent blood to be shed. No, this time he was led astray by the vice of pride.

"I'm an important man," he told himself gloatingly one day. "I rule over a million people—perhaps even more. There isn't a stronger or a more powerful ruler anywhere."

As David reflected on the position which was his, the desire grew strong within him to discover the exact population of Israel—particularly the number of able-bodied men who could be counted upon to lift the sword in battle—and finally he could restrain his curiosity no longer.

"Let a census be taken of all Israel," he commanded. "I must know the exact number of my subjects."

The royal counsellors were horrified. To take a census or to number the people was permitted at rare intervals by the Hebrew law, but only in connection with raising funds for the upkeep of the sanctuary. David seemed to have forgotten the commandment, set forth generations ago by God Himself when speaking to Moses:

"When thou shalt take the sum of the children of Israel according to their number, every one of them shall give a price for their souls to the Lord...."

Knowing that David did not intend to pay the required tax, the counsellors were beside themselves with anxiety.

"Don't do this thing, sire!" they begged. "No good can come from it!"

But David refused to listen. He was an old man now—70 years of age. What harm was there in his knowing the number of the souls over whom he reigned? In glorying in the hundreds of thousands of able-bodied men whom he could send out to battle with a mere wave of his hand?

"Let the people be numbered," he repeated.

So officials went out from Jerusalem into all parts of the kingdom; and, after nearly 10 months of traveling, they brought back the desired information. In the provinces of Israel some 800,000 fighting men paid homage to David, and in the provinces of Juda another 500,000.

The king's eyes glowed with satisfaction. "I *am* a powerful man," he told himself happily. "1,300,000 soldiers! Surely no other ruler can claim so many?"

But it was not long before the king's conscience, more sensitive than that of most men to the workings of good and evil, began to trouble him. What pride he had shown in disregarding God's law and numbering the people! What carelessness in not arranging for the required tax to be paid into the sanctuary! Now there must surely come some new suffering so that atonement should be made to the divine justice without delay. . . .

The prophet Gad confirmed David's fears, declaring that the Lord had spoken to him in prayer, and that in punishment for his sin of pride the king must accept one of three evils: either a famine of seven years or three months of flight from his enemies, or three days of a destroying pestilence.

"Choose," said the prophet sternly.

Sick at heart, David decided upon the last evil. But when three days had passed and some 70,000 people had perished throughout the kingdom, the king's fear grew to agony—particularly when he was permitted to see the terrifying vision of an angel, sword in hand, about to strike the city of Jerusalem!

"Lord, I am the one who has sinned!" he cried, trembling. "The people here, what have they done? Let Your hand, I beseech You, be turned

AN AVENGING ANGEL
WAS STANDING OVER JERUSALEM!

against me, and against my father's house. . . ."

Touched by these words of sincere repentance, God withheld further punishment and informed David through the prophet Gad that his prayer had been heard. Jerusalem would be spared. All that the king need do to complete his atonement was to purchase the threshing floor of a wealthy man named Areuna. Here an altar could be built and sacrifice offered to the Most High.

How eagerly David set about obeying the divine command! And what gratitude filled his heart on the day when he came to attend the dedication of the holy place! No longer was he the proud ruler, boasting of his enormous wealth and power. Now he saw himself for what he was—a poor human creature made out of the slime of the earth, and raised to the dignity of life only by the goodness of God.

David had written a special song for the dedication of the new altar—one which told the touching story of a man overconfident in prosperity, brought low by sickness and misfortune, then saved from death by a merciful Creator. This he now began to sing, in the presence of all the people:

I will extol thee, O Lord, for thou hast upheld me: and hast not made my enemies to rejoice over me.

O Lord my God, I have cried to thee, and thou hast healed me.

Thou hast brought forth, O Lord, my soul from hell: thou hast saved me from them that go down into the pit.

Sing to the Lord, O ye his saints: and give praise to the memory of his holiness.

For wrath is in his indignation; and life in his *good* will.

In the evening weeping shall have place, and in the morning gladness.

And in my abundance I said: I shall never be moved.

O Lord, in thy favour, thou gavest strength to my beauty.

Thou turnedst away thy face from me, and I became troubled.

To thee, O Lord, will I cry: and I will make supplication to my God.

What profit is there in my blood, whilst I go down to corruption?

Shall dust confess to thee, or declare thy truth?

The Lord hath heard, and hath had mercy on me: the Lord became my helper.

Thou hast turned for me my mourning into joy: thou hast cut my sackcloth, and hast compassed me with gladness:

To the end that my glory may sing to thee, and I may not regret: O Lord my God, I will give praise to thee for ever.*

Psalm 29

CHAPTER 18

ADVICE FOR YOUNG SOLOMON

A S THE days passed, David's failing strength brought him to the realization that he had not long to live. In a little while his 19-year-old son Solomon would be reigning in his place. What matter that other sons—Adonias, Jethraam, Samua, Sobab and Nathan—were older and more experienced in warfare? Long ago God had given David to understand that it was Solomon who should succeed to the throne. Under him, and him alone, would Israel prosper.

"And under Solomon will the great temple of Jerusalem be built," thought the aging king happily. "Ah, that I might live to see that glorious sight!"

But well the king realized that this was not to be, and so he contented himself with collecting materials for the temple—stone, iron, brass, marble, cedar wood, gold, silver and precious gems. He also arranged for thousands of skilled craftsmen to cut, polish and otherwise prepare the materials for use.

Yet even as he worked to make the temple of Jerusalem the most beautiful building in all the world, a worthy dwelling place for the Ark of the Covenant, anxiety filled David's soul. Solomon was so young for the great responsibility that soon would be his! And though he was wise beyond his years, and the nation's affairs were in excellent order, the position of a mere boy at the head of a great kingdom was fraught with many dangers. Wicked men might well try to take advantage of his youth and inexperience.

"There's only one way out of the difficulty," David told himself slowly. "From the start Solomon must learn to put his whole trust in God and seek his happiness only in Him. Then when troubles come, he'll know where to turn."

But even as he uttered these words, a shadow crossed David's face. How often during his own lifetime had he determined to root all his desires in God, and presently turned aside to seek his happiness in creatures, in possessions, in worldly amusements! How often had he—able king and leader though he was—become so confused as to mistake *pleasure*, a fleeting delight of the senses, for *joy*, the lasting possession of good!

Suddenly David felt his heart swell with longing. Oh, if Solomon could be spared the wretchedness and evil into which he himself had fallen! If he could learn to keep before him those two important truths—that it is only the just man who can know real peace; that the unjust, no matter what his apparent good fortune, is doomed to misery and failure!

"Lord, give me the right words to explain these

"LORD, HELP ME TO EXPLAIN THINGS
TO SOLOMON..."

things to my son!" begged David earnestly. "Speak, before it is too late. . . ."

Then, as had happened so many times before, divine wisdom began to fill David's heart. Soon it was overflowing into a new song—beautiful, holy, consoling:

> Be not emulous of evildoers; nor envy them that work iniquity.
>
> For they shall shortly wither away as grass, and as the green herbs shall quickly fall.
>
> Trust in the Lord, and do good, and dwell in the land, and thou shalt be fed with its riches.
>
> Delight in the Lord, and he will give thee the requests of thy heart.
>
> Commit thy way to the Lord, and trust in him, and he will do it.
>
> And he will bring forth thy justice as the light, and thy judgment as the noonday. Be subject to the Lord and pray to him.
>
> Envy not the man who prospereth in his way; the man who doth unjust things.
>
> Cease from anger, and leave rage; have no emulation to do evil.
>
> For evildoers shall be cut off: but they that wait upon the Lord, they shall inherit the land.
>
> For yet a little while, and the wicked shall not be: and thou shalt seek his place, and shalt not find it.
>
> But the meek shall inherit the land, and shall delight in abundance of peace.
>
> The sinner shall watch the just man: and shall gnash upon him with his teeth.
>
> But the Lord shall laugh at him: for he foreseeth that his day shall come.

The wicked have drawn out the sword: they have bent their bow.

To cast down the poor and needy, to kill the upright of heart.

Let their sword enter into their own hearts, and let their bow be broken.

Better is a little to the just, than the great riches of the wicked.

For the arms of the wicked shall be broken in pieces; but the Lord strengtheneth the just.

The Lord knoweth the days of the undefiled; and their inheritance shall be for ever.

They shall not be confounded in the evil time; and in the days of famine they shall be filled: because the wicked shall perish.

And the enemies of the Lord, presently after they shall be honoured and exalted, shall come to nothing and vanish like smoke.

The sinner shall borrow, and not pay again; but the just sheweth mercy and shall give.

For such as bless him shall inherit the land: but such as curse him shall perish.

With the Lord shall the steps of a man be directed, and he shall like well his way.

When he shall fall he shall not be bruised, for the Lord putteth his hand under him.

I have been young, and now am old; and I have not seen the just forsaken, nor his seed seeking bread.

He sheweth mercy, and lendeth all the day long; and his seed shall be in blessing.

Decline from evil and do good, and dwell for ever and ever.

For the Lord loveth judgment, and will not forsake his saints: they shall be preserved for ever.

The unjust shall be punished, and the seed of the wicked shall perish.

But the just shall inherit the land, and shall dwell therein for evermore.

The mouth of the just shall meditate wisdom: and his tongue shall speak judgment.

The law of his God is in his heart, and his steps shall not be supplanted.

The wicked watcheth the just man, and seeketh to put him to death.

But the Lord will not leave him in his hands; nor condemn him when he shall be judged.

Expect the Lord and keep his way: and he will exalt thee to inherit the land: when the sinners shall perish thou shalt see.

I have seen the wicked highly exalted, and lifted up like the cedars of Libanus.

And I passed by, and lo, he was not: and I sought him and his place was not found.

Keep innocence, and behold justice: for there are remnants for the peaceable man.

But the unjust shall be destroyed together: the remnants of the wicked shall perish.

But the salvation of the just is from the Lord, and he is their protector in the time of trouble.

And the Lord will help them and deliver them: and he will rescue them from the wicked, and save them, because they have hoped in him.*

*Psalm 36

CHAPTER 19

DAVID SPENDS HIS LAST STRENGTH

D AVID GREW steadily weaker, and soon it was evident that he could not live much longer. The hardships and trials of his 40-year reign (seven years in Hebron and 33 years in Jerusalem) had aged him long before his time.

"Sorrow has also brought him low," whispered his friends knowingly. "Ah, surely there has never been a king to weep so bitterly over his sins?"

But David's trials were not yet over. One day his fourth son, Adonias (the next in line after Absalom) gave a great feast at Zoheleth, a public garden a short distance to the northeast of Jerusalem. Here, surrounded by ambitious friends and followers, he daringly presented himself to the people as their new king.

"My father is old and sickly," he declared. "My brothers are young and inexperienced. But I am ready to serve Israel—if Israel wishes."

There was a murmur of astonishment at this, which quickly changed into whole-hearted approval as Joab, the able general of David's armies, announced in ringing tones that the man before them was certainly the one to rule over Israel. Was he not the oldest of King David's living sons? Was he not a fine soldier—brave, eager, willing—and possessed of an honorable reputation as well?

The high priest Abiathar, who was also present, agreed with everything that Joab said, and soon a wave of enthusiasm was sweeping over the unsuspecting people.

"Adonias is our king!" they shouted eagerly. "May the Lord bless and preserve him!"

"May he know peace and prosperity!"

"May he see his children's children's children!"

"God save our new king!"

"God save King Adonias!"

Of course when word reached David of what was taking place at Zoheleth, he was beside himself with anxiety. What a terrible thing had just happened! For although Adonias was the oldest of the royal sons now living, it had not been he whom God had chosen to be king. Years ago David had learned in prayer that this great honor had been reserved for Solomon alone.

"I must act at once," the king told himself, trembling. "Otherwise, some new and terrible punishment will surely descend upon Jerusalem."

Unmindful of his weakness, David immediately sent for three of his most trusted officials: Sadoc the high priest, Nathan the prophet, and Banaias, a general in the army. The youthful Solomon must be anointed king at once, he declared, and at some distance from the city, so that an imposing procession could make its way through the streets in full view of all the people. The royal bodyguard must be in attendance. Solomon must ride upon David's own mule. There must be music and singing and flags and banners, with a great feast to be held later. And all must be done as speedily as possible, before the happenings at Zoheleth had become generally known among the people.

"Yes, sire," agreed the high priest readily. "But where shall we go? Prince Adonias and his friends are gathered outside the city to the northeast. . . ."

An eager light flickered in David's eyes. If only his aged limbs would support him for one last time, so that he might see his boy anointed with holy oil and proclaimed King of Israel! If only he, too, might take part in the procession! Then slowly he put the thought from him.

"Go to Gihon, in the valley to the west of the city," he said. "That way there will be no confusion. And. . .and one thing more. . . ."

"Yes, sire?"

"Return to the city promptly, so that I may speak with my son—*the king!*"

All was done as David commanded, and with such dispatch that Adonias and his companions were caught unawares. In fact, the feasting at Zoheleth came abruptly to an end as a breathless messenger reported that Solomon, with the blessing of his father, had ascended the throne; that back in Jerusalem the people were now surging through the streets in a whole-hearted demonstration of affection and esteem for their new ruler.

At this unexpected turn of events the merry-makers at Zoheleth realized their danger, and at once began to flee for their lives. Adonias, more fearful than anyone, hastened to the sanctuary to cling to the altar. Here surely he would be safe from his brother's wrath. But in just a little while word came that Solomon had no designs upon his life. Adonias was free to return home at any time. As long as he obeyed the laws of the land, no harm would come to him.

Naturally David rejoiced that the recent uprising had been subdued so quickly and so easily. How terrible if Adonias had been as proud and self-willed as his brother Absalom, and the country had been forced to experience the evils of another civil war! But now all was well, and Solomon was universally accepted as his father's successor.

"God be praised!" David told himself over and over again. "God be praised forever and ever!"

But presently a longing to do more than thank God privately filled the king's heart. If only he might thank Him *publicly*, before all the people gathered together! If only he might stand before them for one last time, urging them to aid his son in the great task of building a glorious temple to the Most High! What if he were old and weak— almost at the point of death? Surely it was a good thing to spend one's last strength in the service of God?

"I will do it," he thought. "*I must do it!*"

Of course everyone realized that any undue exertion would hasten David's death. Nevertheless, an assembly of the people was arranged in the great courtyard before the royal palace. And in a little while, supported by a few trusted servants, David was standing before the chief men of Israel—the princes of the tribes, the leaders of the army, priests, prophets and court officials—ready to deliver his message.

A great silence descended upon the vast gathering as the dying king began to speak. Every ear was strained to catch the feeble voice that was officially presenting the youthful Solomon to his subjects, that begged for loyalty to him and the holy task which would be the first to occupy his attention now that he had ascended the throne—the building of the temple. But when David also told of his own desire to build the temple, of the rejection of his desire by God because of his sins, of his efforts to help by contributing what materials he could, the people wept. What a moving sight it was—this old man in his royal robes, staggering, scarcely able to speak, using his last strength to accuse himself of the sins which prayer and sacrifice must surely have atoned for long ago. . . .

David, however, was forgetful of himself. His mind was intent on one thing: that the people might share with him in the great work of raising a temple to God's glory.

"I have given what I could," he said, his voice beginning to break with weariness. "Now if any man is willing, let him also offer to the Lord. . ."

Suddenly the silence was no more. A wave of enthusiasm swept through the crowd, and in an

eager chorus the people began to declare their gifts.
"Five measures of gold!"
"Ten measures of silver!"
"Thirty measures of brass!"
"Fifty measures of iron!"
Wood, stone, marble, precious gems—the list
seemed endless. And boundless was the joy of the
people as they announced their offerings. For well
they knew they were not merely giving *things* to God.
They were giving *themselves,* their hearts and wills,
in a great demonstration of love. And even as they
gave they were reaping in contentment a hundredfold.
"Truly, it is always this way when we give to
God," thought David, tears shining in his eyes. "He
cannot be outdone in generosity." And as he pon-
dered the glorious thought, suddenly there was
holy music in the king's heart, and fresh strength
within his tired limbs. Stretching out his arms, he
faced the people and began to sing a song which
they had never heard before—a song of gratitude
and praise:

> Blessed art thou, O Lord, God of Israel our
> father, from eternity to eternity.
> Thine, O Lord, is magnificence and power, and
> splendor and glory and majesty. For all things that
> are in heaven and on earth are thine: thine is the
> kingdom, O Lord, and thine is the ruler who is
> exalted above all.
> Riches and honor are from thee, and by thy
> dominion thou rulest all things. And in thy hand
> is strength and power; and in thy hand it is to make
> great and to give strength unto all.

"BLESSED ART THOU, O LORD, GOD OF ISRAEL..."

Now therefore, our God, we honor thee and we praise thy glorious name.*

A reverent hush fell upon the great assembly as David sang his song. Then suddenly the courtyard before the royal palace was echoing with triumphant sound as the people also raised their voices in heartfelt tribute to the Most High:

Praise ye the Lord in his holy places: praise ye him in the firmament of his power.

Praise ye him for his mighty acts: praise ye him according to the multitude of his greatness.

Praise him with sound of trumpet: praise him with psaltery and harp.

Praise him with timbrel and choir: praise him with strings and organs.

Praise him on high sounding cymbals: praise him on cymbals of joy: let every spirit praise the Lord. Alleluia.**

Smiling, at peace, David let himself be led away. The old weakness was upon him again, but this did not matter. He had done what he had set out to do. He had spent his last strength in the service of God.

"Now let me die," he asked silently, a mist rising before his eyes so that he could scarcely see. "Let me sleep with my fathers...."

*Canticle of David
**Psalm 150

CHAPTER 20

THE MYSTERIOUS FUTURE KINGDOM

D AVID HAD been right in his belief that his time on earth was ended. Very soon, surrounded by his grieving household, he had breathed his last.

As the long-expected announcement of his death was made throughout the city, the people bowed their heads in reverent tribute. What a wonderful ruler they had had! Poet, musician, soldier, statesman—David had been all of these, and to a degree of surpassing excellence.

"May God give him rest!" was the earnest prayer that went up from every heart as his body was placed in the royal tomb on Mount Sion. "And may He bless the young King Solomon...."

Of course Solomon was encouraged by the loyalty and affection of his people. Nevertheless, he could not help but be a little fearful of the future, and daily he called to mind the words with which his dying father had so earnestly counseled him:

"And thou my son Solomon, know the God of thy father, and serve him with a perfect heart, and a willing mind: for the Lord searcheth all hearts, and understandeth all the thoughts of minds. If thou seek him, thou shalt find him: but if thou forsake him, he will cast thee off for ever!"

There were other words to recall, too—words which David had spoken concerning the Messias, the great King whom one day God would raise up from among the Hebrew people to rule the world. Oh, how exalted the Promised One would be! How good, wise, powerful, just...

"There will be no end to His kingdom," Solomon told himself in awed tones. Then, even as he reflected upon the stupendous thought, a mighty longing filled the young man's soul. "Oh, if I might have a worthy reign, too!" he whispered. "If I might serve my people with justice, so that there could be lasting peace throughout Israel!"

Slowly Solomon got to his knees, asking humbly for guidance in the difficult task of ruling Israel. Then, as he arose, prophetic words of his father David came to mind—prophecies referring to Solomon's upcoming reign, but especially describing the future reign of God's Anointed One. Yes, these holy words told of the Messias, who one day would be born of the Royal House of David, descended from King Solomon himself, down through many generations...to a Virgin named Mary.

> Give to the king thy judgment, O God: and to the king's son thy justice:
> To judge thy people with justice, and thy poor with judgment.

"OH, IF I MIGHT HAVE A WORTHY REIGN, TOO!"

Let the mountains receive peace for the people: and the hills justice.

He shall judge the poor of the people, and he shall save the children of the poor: and he shall humble the oppressor.

And he shall continue with the sun, and before the moon, throughout all generations.

He shall come down like rain upon the fleece; and as showers falling gently upon the earth.

In his days shall justice spring up, and abundance of peace, till the moon be taken away.

And he shall rule from sea to sea, and from the river unto the ends of the earth.

Before him the Ethiopians shall fall down: and his enemies shall lick the ground.

The kings of Tharsis and the islands shall offer presents: the kings of the Arabians and of Saba shall bring gifts:

And all kings of the earth shall adore him: all nations shall serve him.

For he shall deliver the poor from the mighty: and the needy that had no helper.

He shall spare the poor and needy: and he shall save the souls of the poor.

He shall redeem their souls from usuries and iniquity: and their names shall be honourable in his sight.

And he shall live, and to him shall be given of the gold of Arabia, for him they shall always adore: they shall bless him all the day.

And there shall be a firmament on the earth on the tops of mountains, above Libanus shall the fruit thereof be exalted: and they of the city shall flourish like the grass of the earth.

Let his name be blessed for evermore: his name continueth before the sun.

And in him shall all the tribes of the earth be blessed: all nations shall magnify him.

Blessed be the Lord, the God of Israel, who alone doth wonderful things.

And blessed be the name of his majesty for ever: and the whole earth shall be filled with his majesty. So be it. So be it.*

St. Meinrad, Indiana
Feast of the Assumption of the Blessed Virgin Mary
August 15, 1947

Psalm 71

Also by the same author . . .

6 <u>MORE</u> GREAT CATHOLIC
BOOKS FOR CHILDREN
. . . and for all young people ages 10 to 100!!

1200 SAINT THOMAS AQUINAS—The Story of "The Dumb Ox." 81 pp. PB. 16 Illus. Impr. The remarkable story of how St. Thomas, called in school "The Dumb Ox," became the greatest Catholic teacher ever.   6.00

1201 SAINT CATHERINE OF SIENA—The Story of the Girl Who Saw Saints in the Sky. 65 pp. PB. 13 Illus. The amazing life of the most famous Catherine in the history of the Church.   5.00

1202 SAINT HYACINTH OF POLAND—The Story of The Apostle of the North. 189 pp. PB. 16 Illus. Impr. Shows how the holy Catholic Faith came to Poland, Lithuania, Prussia, Scandinavia and Russia.   11.00

1203 SAINT MARTIN DE PORRES—The Story of The Little Doctor of Lima, Peru. 122 pp. PB. 16 Illus. Impr. The incredible life and miracles of this black boy who became a great saint.   7.00

1204 SAINT ROSE OF LIMA—The Story of The First Canonized Saint of the Americas. 132 pp. PB. 13 Illus. Impr. The remarkable life of the little Rose of South America.   8.00

1205 PAULINE JARICOT—Foundress of the Living Rosary and The Society for the Propagation of the Faith. 244 pp. PB. 21 Illus. Impr. The story of a rich young girl and her many spiritual adventures.   13.00

1206 ALL 6 BOOKS ABOVE (Reg. 50.00)   THE SET: 40.00

Prices subject to change.

U.S. & CAN. POST./HDLG.: $1-$10, add $2; $10.01-$20, add $3;
$20.01-$30, add $4; $30.01-$50, add $5; $50.01-$75, add $6; $75.01-up, add $7.

At your Bookdealer or direct from the Publisher.
Call Toll Free 1-800-437-5876

More books by the same author . . .

8 MORE GREAT CATHOLIC BOOKS FOR CHILDREN

. . . and for all young people ages 10 to 100!!

1230 SAINT PAUL THE APOSTLE—The Story of the Apostle to the Gentiles. 231 pp. PB. 23 Illus. Impr. The many adventures that met St. Paul in the early Catholic Church.   13.00

1231 SAINT BENEDICT—The Story of the Father of the Western Monks. 158 pp. PB. 19 Illus. Impr. The life and great miracles of the man who planted monastic life in Europe.   8.00

1232 SAINT MARGARET MARY—And the Promises of the Sacred Heart of Jesus. 224 pp. PB. 21 Illus. Impr. The wonderful story of remarkable gifts from Heaven. Includes St. Claude de la Colombière.   11.00

1233 SAINT DOMINIC—Preacher of the Rosary and Founder of the Dominican Order. 156 pp. PB. 19 Illus. Impr. The miracles, trials and travels of one of the Church's most famous saints.   8.00

Continued on next page . . .

At your Bookdealer or direct from the Publisher.
Call Toll Free 1-800-437-5876

1234 KING DAVID AND HIS SONGS—A Story of the Psalms. 138 pp. PB. 23 Illus. Impr. The story of the shepherd boy who became a warrior, a hero, a fugitive, a king, and more. 8.00

1235 SAINT FRANCIS SOLANO—Wonder-Worker of the New World and Apostle of Argentina and Peru. 205 pp. PB. 19 Illus. Impr. The story of St. Francis' remarkable deeds in Spain and South America. 11.00

1236 SAINT JOHN MASIAS—Marvelous Dominican Gatekeeper of Lima, Peru. 156 pp. PB. 14 Illus. Impr. The humble brother who fought the devil and freed a million souls from Purgatory. 8.00

1237 BLESSED MARIE OF NEW FRANCE—The Story of the First Missionary Sisters in Canada. 152 pp. PB. 18 Illus. Impr. The story of a wife, mother and nun—and her many adventures in pioneer Canada. 9.00

1238 ALL 8 BOOKS ABOVE (Reg. 76.00)   THE SET: 60.00

Prices subject to change.

MARY FABYAN WINDEATT

Mary Fabyan Windeatt could well be called the "storyteller of the saints," for such indeed she was. And she had a singular talent for bringing out doctrinal truths in her stories, so that without even realizing it, young readers would see the Catholic catechism come to life in the lives of the saints.

Mary Fabyan Windeatt wrote at least 21 books for children, plus the text of about 28 Catholic story coloring books. At one time there were over 175,000 copies of her books on the saints in circulation. She contributed a regular "Children's Page" to the monthly Dominican magazine, *The Torch*.

Miss Windeatt began her career of writing for the Catholic press around age 24. After graduating from San Diego State College in 1934, she had gone to New York looking for work in advertising. Not finding any, she sent a story to a Catholic magazine. It was accepted—and she continued to write. Eventually Miss Windeatt wrote for 33 magazines, contributing verse, articles, book reviews and short stories.

Having been born in 1910 in Regina, Saskatchewan, Canada, Mary Fabyan Windeatt received the Licentiate of Music degree from Mount Saint Vincent College, in Halifax, Nova Scotia at age 17. With her family she moved to San Diego in that same year, 1927. In 1940 Miss Windeatt received an A.M. degree from Columbia University. Later, she lived with her mother near St. Meinrad's Abbey, St. Meinrad, Indiana. Mary Fabyan Windeatt died on November 20, 1979.

(Much of the above information is from Catholic Authors: Contemporary Biographical Sketches 1930-1947, *ed. by Matthew Hoehn, O.S.B., B.L.S., St. Mary's Abbey, Newark, N.J., 1957.)*